AF345343

guided by the divine light

Vol. I
Guided by the Divine Light

Notes from Lectures of Shaykh
Sidi Mohamed Faouzi al-Karkari

Translated by Mohamed Wael Draoui
Edited by Ahmed Mobeen & Faizal Allie

L·7 LES 7 LECTURES

A CELESTIAL ORGANIZATION   BUILT ON EARTH
AL KARKARI
INSTITUTE
BY SHAYKH MOHAMED FAOUZI AL-KARKARI

أعوذ بالله من الشيطان الرجيم

بسم الله الرحمن الرحيم

بسم الله الرحمن الرحيم

بسم الله الرحمن الرحيم

بسم الله

بسم الله

بسم الله

الله

الله

الله

ولا حول ولا قوة إلا بالله العلي العظيم

Table of Contents

*This work would never have seen the Light without
Sidi Shaykh. If something is wrong it will be from
ourselves, and everything that is correct
is from Sidi Shaykh.*

Introduction

In the Name of God, the All-Merciful,
the Ever-Merciful.

The lectures of Sidi Shaykh Mohamed Faouzi al-Karkari,
may Allah sanctify his secret, shine as a guiding Light for
his disciples on their spiritual journey. These luminous
teachings take the form of question-and-answer sessions,
where the Shaykh addresses questions from his disciples
regarding their direct visions of Light, dream visions, and
any other matters that interest them.

This book is a compilation of notes derived from Sidi
Shaykh's responses to his disciples' questions. In certain
notes, the translation includes multiple answers from the
same lecture to summarize the key concepts discussed, while
in others, a single response is explored in depth.

In our translation, we strive to capture the essence and
authenticity of Sidi Shaykh's teachings, preserving the
cadence and phrasing of his discourse while ensuring clar-
ity and accessibility for readers. While our aim is not to
provide a word-for-word rendition, we endeavor to convey
the luminous subtle flow inherent in Sidi Shaykh's words.

Lecture 1.
November 22, 2022

*

The night prayer (*qiyam al-layl*)

Q: A disciple asked how to perform the night prayer *(qiyam al-layl)* during the last third of the night.

Sidi Shaykh gave a detailed response consisting of five steps: preparation, ablution, prayers, remembrance (*dhikr*), and post-*qiyam* practices.

Part 1: Preparation

For this initial part, Sidi Shaykh recommended the following steps:

- ► Calculate the length of the last third of the night based on the timing of the Maghrib and Fajr prayers.
- ► Prepare the place for *qiyam al-layl* before going to bed.
- ► Recite the following invocations when waking up for *qiyam al-layl,* before leaving the bed:
  La ilaha illallah, wahdahu la sharika lahu, lahul-mulk, wa lahul-hamd, yuhyi wa yumitu, wa huwa hayyun la yamutu, biyadihil-khayr, wa huwa ʿala kulli shayin qadir.

Subhanallahi wal-hamdulillahi, wa la ilaha illallah,
wallahu akbar, wa la hawla wa la quwwata illa billah.
Tidy the bed before beginning the night prayers.

Part 2: Ablutions

Sidi Shaykh emphasized the importance of maintaining a state of presence with Allah throughout performing the ritual purification or ablutions. One should:

- Direct oneself toward the *qibla*.
- Use a bucket for ablutions rather than the open faucet.
- Wash each part of the body three times.
- Avoid wasting water.

After completing ablutions, it is advised to recite the *Shahada*, bearing witness to the oneness of Allah. From this point forward, one should refrain from speaking even to oneself and start reciting *istighfar* in a low voice until reaching the prayer area for *qiyam al-layl*.

In order to emphasize the importance of using a vessel of water for ablutions rather than the open faucet, Sidi Shaykh shared an anecdote about a certain Sufi Shaykh. The Shaykh was approached by a person who wanted to learn how to perform ablutions. The Shaykh asked him to get a bucket. With the bucket in hand, he showed the person how to do ablutions while he watched. The person then asked: "What about the mandatory (fard) and optional (*sunnah*) acts of ablutions?" The Shaykh replied: "They are all in the bucket."

Part 3: Prayers

Sidi Shaykh mentioned the importance of performing some sets (*raka'at*) of supererogatory prayers before starting remembrance. He recommended the following:

- Recite Surah al-Ikhlas 100 times. This can be divided into multiple prayer units, ranging from two to ten. For example, if one performs ten units, he would recite the Surah 10 times per unit, whereas if one performs only two units, he would recite the Surah 50 times per unit. It is crucial to adhere to the initial intention set at the beginning of the prayer of how many units to perform and avoid any alteration midway.
- It is also suggested to recite prayers audibly, as this can cultivate a deeper sense of presence during prayer. One should also concentrate on the place of prostration as it helps to witness the Divine Light.

Part 4: Remembrance (*dhikr*)

Sidi Shaykh advised various formulas of remembrance:

- Start with one hundred repetitions of seeking forgiveness, *istighfar*, followed by one hundred recitations of "*Subhanallah walhamdulillah wala ilaha illa Allah wallahu akbar*"
- Invoke the Name "Allah" for at least one hour.

[Note: This only applies to disciples who have been granted explicit permission from the Shaykh to invoke the Name "Allah", to those physically present in the Zawiya and participating in congregational *dhikr*, and to disciples who follow Sidi Shaykh via livestream while he is invoking the Name "Allah". If the previous conditions do not apply to the individual, he should engage in *dhikr* of *istighfar*.]

- Upon completion of the invocation of the Name "Allah" or *istighfar*, perform supplications for oneself and praise God with, "*Alhamdulillah wa shukru lillah*" one hundred times to express gratitude to God for providing the strength to engage in this *qiyam al-layl.*

▸ Finally send salutations and blessings upon the Prophet ﷺ.

Sidi Shaykh recommended practicing remembrance by sitting facing the *qibla* while in a clean (*tahir*) and dark place. It is also important to close the eyes and clear the mind of thoughts to focus and witness the Light.

Part 5: Post-*qiyam* practices

▸ After completing *qiyam al-layl*, it is advised to return to sleep to wake up approximately five minutes before the Fajr prayer. At this point, one should repeat the ablutions, perform two units of prayer, and patiently await the call to prayer.

▸ Following the call to prayer, Fajr and Subh prayers are to be performed.

▸ Recite the litany (*al-wird*): Practicing the morning litany.

▸ Embrace the sunrise: For those who find the strength, Sidi Shaykh highly encourages, to remain engaged in remembrance until sunrise (*shuruq*).

▸ Sidi Shaykh mentioned that the alternating sleep pattern in the night supplies the body with a significant surge of energy to reach sunrise easily. He also stated that reaching sunrise while doing *dhikr* and praying two units of prayers without moving from one's place is equivalent to undertaking a *Hajj* and *Umrah* pilgrimage with the Prophet ﷺ.

Sidi Shaykh concluded saying that this is the proper way to perform *qiyam al-layl*. It is important to note that there is no strict obligation to follow this specific method. For example, at the Zawiya, the program is adapted to various categories of people. However, when practicing at home, everyone has the flexibility to create his own program.

Lecture 2.
November 23, 2022

*

The vision of the example is higher
than the vision of objects

Q: A disciple stated that in a direct vision (*mushahada*), he witnessed images of multiple objects.

Sidi Shaykh said that in direct visions the disciple should not focus on the images themselves. Instead, he should focus on the Light because that is more important than the images. When a disciple has a direct vision of an image, such as a bird or a rose, he should seek the message or the characteristics within these images. He should then return to focusing on the example (*mathal*) of Allah's Light which is represented by the niche (*al-mishkat*), the lamp (*al-misbah*), the glass (*al-zujaja*), and the shining star (*al-kawkab al-durri*).

*

Attaining love for the Shaykh

Q: A disciple asked how one can attain love for the Shaykh.

Sidi Shaykh explained that it is not the job of the Shaykh to teach the disciple how to love his Shaykh. It is up to the disciple to know how to treat his Shaykh. He added that if one loves the Shaykh, he loves Sainthood (*al-wilaya*), and if he hates the Shaykh, he hates Sainthood.

Sidi Shaykh also said that before he became a *Wali*, a Friend of God, no one claimed to love the Shaykh. But when he became a *Wali*, everyone came to him and claimed to love him. This proves that they love the secrets (*asrar*) he possesses. This type of love is incomplete, the disciple should love his Shaykh for his Essence.

Sidi Shaykh finished his response by saying that there isn't a process or a law for love, it is a subtle flow (*sarayan*) from God that one cannot put words on it.

*

The significance of the pronouns used by al-Khidr

Q: In verses 79 through 82 of Surah al-Kahf, Sayyiduna al-Khidr, peace be upon him, explained to Sayyiduna Musa, peace be upon him, the reasons behind the three acts he did. He said: **"As for the ship, it belonged to indigent people who worked the sea. I desired to damage it. And as for**

the young boy, his parents were believers and we feared that he would make them suffer much through rebellion and disbelief. So, we desired that their Lord give them in exchange one who is better than him in purity, and nearer to mercy. And as for the wall, it belonged to two orphan boys in the city, and beneath it was a treasure belonging to them. Their father was righteous, and thy Lord desired that they should reach their maturity and extract their treasure, as a mercy from thy Lord. And I did not do this upon my own."[1] Sayyiduna al-Khidr, peace be upon him, used the pronoun "I" in verse 79, "we" in verse 81, and the word "Lord" in verse 82. A disciple asked about the significance of this change of pronoun at each step of the wayfaring of Sayyiduna Musa with Sayyiduna al-Khidr, peace be upon them.

Sidi Shaykh explained that the use of the pronoun "I" in informing about the ship's damage, demonstrates that the Shaykh can define the foundations of his Tariqa on his own. As for killing the soul (*al-nafs*) of the disciple, it is as if it is a duality between the Shaykh and his Lord. That's why al-Khidr used the pronoun "we" in killing the boy. At the final stage, al-Khidr used the word "Lord" which can be associated with the pronoun him (*huwa*). This proves that hiding the treasure concerns Allah. The Shaykh is only hiding what Allah already hidden.

....

1   Quran 18:79-82.

*

Sufi diets

Q: A disciple asked Sidi Shaykh about the best diet to follow for their wayfaring (*suluk*) and education of the soul (*tarbiyat al-nafs*).

Sidi Shaykh referred to the Hadith of the Prophet ﷺ: "We are a people who do not eat until we are hungry. And if we eat, we do not eat to our full."[2] Sidi Shaykh added that historically Sufis practiced multiple diets. Some did not eat meat and all other animal products, while others only ate cereals. There were also those who lived only with water as their only food. Sidi Shaykh explained that in the Tariqa Karkariya, there are no restrictions in terms of diet and food for the disciple. He referred to a teaching of his own Shaykh, Moulay al-Hassan, God have mercy on him: "Eat what you want but practice your *dhikr*".

*

The significance of "neither of the East nor of the West"

Q: A disciple questioned Sidi Shaykh about the significance of the Blessed Olive Tree (*shajarah mubaraka*)

....

2   Al-Halabi, Nur ad-Din. *Sirat al-Halbiya*. Vol. 3, Page: 299.

being neither of the East nor of the West in verse 35 of Surah al-Nur. For instance, does this signify that the tree is in every direction? Additionally, could it be symbolically represented by the Arabic letter '*alif*' or the Arabic numeral 'one'?

Sidi Shaykh said that this part of the verse means that the Olive Tree is non-directional. Thus, it is incorrect to say that the Blessed Olive Tree is in every direction. Sidi Shaykh also referred to the Hadith of the Prophet ﷺ in which he explained that the Quran is a cord extending from heaven to the earth which represents the letter '*alif*'. If one was to represent the Blessed Olive Tree, it can be represented as a dot on top of the '*alif*'. The '*alif*' represents the attribute, and the dot represents the secret of the Essence.

If one is looking for directionality, then he should consider the Light of the heavens and the earth, not the Blessed Olive Tree. That's why the path starts with a niche, which is the *Ha* of Divine Identity (*ha' al-huwiyya*), then a lamp and a glass, which are the *Lam* of contraction (*lam al-qabd*) and the *Lam* of gnosis (*lam al-ma'rifa*), then, the disciple reaches the scission (*al-fasl*), where he stays under the tree and never leaves until he becomes purely for Allah (*lillah*). That's how the disciple succeeds. But when he tries to catch the '*alif*', he fails and the '*alif*' catches the '*lam*' to form the word "no" (*la*), which is the association of the letter '*alif*' and the letter '*lam*' in Arabic, and the disciple loses everything.

The *alif* is reserved for the Elite (*'itra*) of *Ahl al-Bayt*, if the disciple claims he is the '*alif*' then he loses the '*lam*' and becomes a god (*ilah*), which was the pretension of Pharaoh.

Lecture 3.
November 24, 2022

*

Witnessing the Divine Light in prostration (*sujud*)

Q: A disciple remarked that the best position for him to see the Light is in prostration (*sujud*).

Sidi Shaykh explained that seeing the Light is equivalent to being present with Allah. The secret is not in the disciple himself, his place, or his position, but rather in his connection and presence with Allah. If he is preoccupied with other thoughts, he is in a state of heedlessness (*ghafla*), otherwise, he is present with Allah.

Sidi Shaykh added that one must witness the Light not only in prostration but also in different states, starting from *dhikr* with closed eyes, and progressing through prayers until reaching a state where one can walk with the Light among people in the markets (*al-aswaq*).

*

Think less of (*istahqir*) yourself and exalt others

Q: In one of his aphorisms, Sidi Shaykh says: "Think less of (*istahqir*) yourself and exalt others". A disciple asked how to actualize this aphorism (*hikma*).

Sidi Shaykh explained that when the disciple repents, he should forget his past whether it was good or bad. He should forget about his good and bad deeds and only engage in remembrance (*dhikr*). Once he begins to clearly witness the example of Allah's Light which is the niche, the lamp, the glass, and the shining star, and has many direct visions of Light, he can then begin humiliating himself and magnifying others by recalling his past bad deeds.

*

Interacting well with family through the Divine Light

Q: A disciple asked about how he should interact with his family once in the Tariqa.

Sidi Shaykh emphasized the importance of interacting with family well. He mentioned that if one's soul (*al-nafs*) has rights over him, what to say about family relatives? Sidi Shaykh added that Allah's Light is a secret within the disciple and he should use it in his interactions. For instance, when interacting with his wife, treating her kindly and communicating with her. One should intend his actions and conversations with her to be for the sake of Allah (*lillah*). This approach transforms the disciple's interactions with his wife into acts of worship (*'ibadah*). Additionally, if he is able to see the Light with open eyes, he should try to see the Light on her face, on her body, etc.

Sidi Shaykh added that this is a general approach to deal with family members, but everyone understands the specific dynamics within his own family, including his children. For example, when it comes to children, one should treat them as friends, sharing problems and engaging in conversations with them. Children should not be used just to serve their parents.

Sidi Shaykh concluded this part by saying that in the case of conflict with relatives, one should always put oneself in the position of the oppressed, not the oppressor, and leave the matter to God.

*

The variation of the moon's size

Q: A disciple asked about the significance and the impact of the variation of the size of the moon in the direct vision of Light (*mushahada*).

Sidi Shaykh mentioned that when the moon becomes full (*qamar badri*), it indicates the birth of the child of meanings (*tifl al-maʿani*). The child of meanings represents the perfect person (*al-insan al-kamil*) within the disciple.

Sidi Shaykh added that if one were to project this in the physical realm (*mulk*), it takes fifteen days for the moon to reach fullness. Before reaching its fullness, the moon is just a crescent (*hilal*). This crescent takes seven days to become fully clear, but during the initial seven days, its intensity is quite low. This pattern aligns with the menstrual cycle, as it takes nearly seven days to prepare for fertilization, reaching readiness by the fifteenth day of the cycle.

It is the same for the disciple. He has the same period for fertilization. In the first fifteen days, he is preparing the fetus of the child of meanings (*tifl al-ma'ani*) until the fifteenth day when the Light becomes a full moon. Then, the growth of the fetus is complete.

So, in the first seven days, when the crescent isn't fully clear, the disciple resembles a menstruating woman. He does not fulfill prayers and obligations, remaining submerged in darkness. However, after these initial seven days, he should become conscious of his actions and aware of his faculties (*jawarih*) until the fifteenth day, meaning when the Light becomes a full moon and he becomes the child of meanings. At this stage, he will focus his work on turning his sight into Light, his hand into Light, his foot into Light, etc.

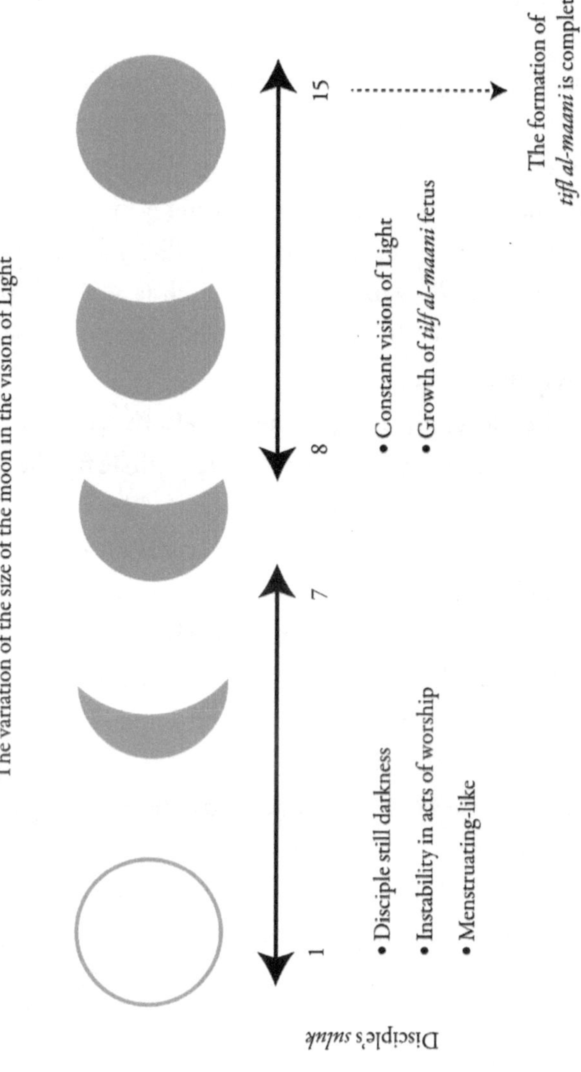

The variation of the size of the moon in the vision of Light
15
8
7
1
Constant vision of Light
Growth of tifl al-maani fetus
The formation of tifl al-maani is completed
Disciple still darkness
Instability in acts of worship
Menstruating-like
Disciple's suluk

Sidi Shaykh added that once the fetus is completely formed, the Shaykh enters the disciple to the spiritual seclusion (*al-kholwa*) and reveals the Secret (*al-sirr*) to him. The disciple leaves the *kholwa* as a whole new person in the same old body. After the birth of the child of meanings comes the period of breastfeeding. The Shaykh feeds the disciple for two cycles. Breastfeeding is knowledge, as the Prophet ﷺ interprets milk as knowledge. Hence, attending lectures (*mudhakarat*) of the Shaykh is an obligation for the disciple. Without attending these lectures, the moon slowly disappears.

Therefore, the disciple must stay in the companionship (*suhba*) of the Shaykh for two cycles until he finishes breastfeeding, just like a baby being breastfed for two full years. During this period, the Shaykh imparts knowledge to the disciple. It is as if there are two breasts, one for jurisprudence (*shari'a*) and the other one for the Divine truth (*haqiqa*) with the Shaykh alternating between them. Then, the Shaykh changes the type of food for the disciple. He applies the Prophet's ﷺ Hadith where he advises to play with children until they are seven years old. Thus, the Shaykh plays with the disciple until he empties all that he has inside him.

Sidi Shaykh added that when the disciple leaves spiritual seclusion, it is an entirely new world for him. Sidi Shaykh referred to verse 12 of Surah al-Talaq **"God it is Who created the seven heavens, and from the earth the like thereof."**[3] In the spiritual seclusion, the Shaykh gathers for the disciple

....

3   Quran 65:12.

the seven heavens, and throughout the rest of the disciple's companionship with him, the Shaykh will do the same with the earth.

Sidi Shaykh added that the earth whereupon humans live is the first earth, and the sky that one sees in the physical realm (*mulk*) is its roof. The Shaykh created for the disciple another heaven, so he needs to also create another earth for him. Living on one earth with two different heavens is impossible.

In the same response, Sidi Shyakh added that when one attempts to traverse through the atmosphere, he will find guards protecting the heavens. He referred to verse 33 of Surah al-Rahman: **"O company of jinn and men, if you are able to pass beyond the regions of the heavens and the earth, then pass, you shall not pass, save by a warrant."**[4] [Note: In this translation, the word "warrant" is employed as an interpretation to the original Arabic word "sultan". In the rest of his answer, Sidi Shaykh uses the original term "sultan" as found in the Arabic version of the verse.]

In verse 35 Allah says: **"A flash of fire and molten brass shall be sent against you, and you shall not prevail."**[5]

Sidi Shaykh explained that the regions of the heavens (*aqtar al-samawat*) mentioned in the verse, resemble holes or niches in the heavens from where one can pass through. To pass through these niches, one needs the Sultan, which is the Shaykh.

. . . .

4   Quran 55:33.
5   Quran 55:35.

When the Shaykh gives the pledge of allegiance (*al-bay'ah*) to the disciple, he opens for him a hole to pass through the heavens. If the disciple attempts to enter from other places, he will get only fire. That's why Sayyiduna Ali, may Allah honor his face, is the door of the city of knowledge, one must follow the Sultan and disregard everything else.

Sidi Shaykh added that the earth's roof is guarded and filled with flames of fire. Within this roof, there are openings through which one can pass by following the Sultan. He added that when one passes through these openings, the first heaven will be split apart and become like a rose. Sidi Shaykh referred to verse 37 and 38 of Surah al-Rahman: **"When the sky splits apart, and it becomes a rose, like paint. So which of your Lord's marvels will you deny?"**[6]

In the same context, Sidi Shaykh explained some verses from Surah al-Jinn. He started with verse 8: **"We reached out to Heaven and found it filled with mighty sentries and flaming stars."** Sidi Shaykh emphasized that the fire and the flaming stars come from hell, not from the sun.

In the next verse, Allah mentions: **"We used to sit in places thereof to listen, but whosoever listens now finds a flaming star lying in wait for him."**[7] Sidi Shaykh explained that since the word "listening" is mentioned in the verse, it implies the presence of an ear. He clarified that disciples are still unable to perceive Divine sounds (*hawatif*) during *dhikr*. The Shaykh has not yet permitted this; the door

....

6   Quran 55:37-38.
7   Quran 72:8.

remains closed. Therefore, it is useless for the disciple to come to the Shaykh and tell him that during *dhikr* he heard something.

Sidi Shaykh added that at the beginning of the verse, the word "places" is used. Before the birth of the Prophet ﷺ, there were places or positions available for anyone who reached the first heaven, but after his birth ﷺ, guards were placed to protect these places which became reserved for the Prophet and *Ahl al-Bayt* ﷺ.

Sidi Shaykh mentioned verse 10 from the same Surah: **"We do not know whether evil is desired for those upon the earth, or whether their Lord desires guidance for them."**[8] Sidi Shaykh emphasized that when one passes through and takes a place, seeing the flames of fire sent from above, he will think that the earth is all burned. Sidi Shaykh described the earth as a small sphere surrounded by fire or a fish in a sea of fire.

In verse 11 of Surah al-Jinn Allah says: **"Some among us are righteous, and some among us are otherwise; we are on paths divided."**[9] Sidi Shaykh explained that people are different, what they have in common is their need for the Sultan.

Sidi Shaykh finished by saying that beyond the atmosphere, there is high-temperature material that burns whoever penetrates except for the ones who found the Sultan because they enter through the gate of the Dot (*al-nuqta*).

....

8   Quran 72:10.
9   Quran 72:11.

Allah gave the Sultan this power not because of his person but because of the secret within him and made him the gate. In this context, the Prophet ﷺ said: "I am the city of knowledge and Ali is its gate."[10]

....

10   Al-Nishapuri, al-Hakim. *Al-Mustadrak ʿala al-Sahihayn*. Vol. 3, Page: 126.

Lecture 4.
November 3, 2022

*

Imitation (*taqlid*) vs Annihilation (*fana'*)

Q: The difference between imitation of the Shaykh and annihilation (*fana'*) in the Shaykh.

Sidi Shaykh said that most of the disciples imitate the Shaykh in his actions, words, etc. However, even their imitation is incomplete; the disciples selectively choose parts of the Shaykh that they like, imitate him, and consider this as annihilation. This is completely wrong, explained Sidi Shaykh, even if the disciple completely imitates the Shaykh he is still in the station of faith (*maqam al-iman*).

The Prophet ﷺ explained the difference between imitation and annihilation with two different Hadiths. In the first Hadith, he said: "My companions are like stars, whichever of them you use as a guide, you'll be rightly guided."[11] This Hadith concerns people of the station of faith. They copy

....

11   Al-Suyuti, Jalal al-Din. *Takhrij Ahadith al-Shifa*. Page, 193.

41

the Prophet's ﷺ *Sunnah* from his companions and they are still rightly guided.

People of the station of excellence (*maqam al-ihsan*) are concerned by the Hadith of Sayyiduna Umar, peace be upon him, when he said: "O Messenger of Allah, you're more beloved to me than everything but myself." The Prophet ﷺ said: "No, by the one in whose hand is my soul, until I am more beloved to you than yourself."[12] So, annihilation in the Prophet ﷺ is by loving him more than oneself. It is the same for the disciple with his Shaykh, he should love him more than anyone else until he loves him more than himself.

The first Hadith about following the companions can be linked to jurisprudence (*shari'a*), the station of faith and imitation. The second one can be linked to the Divine truth (*haqiqa*), the station of excellence, and annihilation.

When the disciple is with the Shaykh, he knows in which station the disciple is. If he is from the people of the station of faith, the Shaykh will talk to him about acts, and about faith, not about secrets and knowledge, this is reserved for the people of the station of excellence.

When the Prophet ﷺ said: "I am the city of knowledge and Ali is its gate"[13], he meant that one should realize annihilation in the gate to pass and enter the city, one cannot pass with his soul (*nafs*). Sidi Shaykh added that when one witnesses the Divine Light, he should not think that he has realized the knowledge included in this Light. For exam-

....

12 *Sahih Bukhari* #6632.
13 Al-Nishapuri, al-Hakim. *Al-Mustadrak 'ala al-Sahihayn*. Vol. 3, Page: 126.

ple, if one sees the moon in the physical realm, he would describe it as a white disc. However, someone who landed on the moon may describe it as a place that contains volcanic rocks. It is indeed true that Sufis assert that whoever attains vision possesses knowledge. In reality, when one experiences the vision of Light, he attains *'ayn al-ma'rifa*, but when one enters the city of knowledge, he comes to realize *haqq al-ma'rifa*.

Sidi Shaykh explained further that when one enters the city of knowledge, he doesn't get all the knowledge, but the part where the Shaykh gave him access. For example, if three people land on the earth: the first in the north pole, the second in a forest, and the third in a desert. Each of them will give a particular description of the earth. The first one will describe it as a planet covered by ice, the second one will describe it as a planet covered by trees, and the third one will describe it as a desert planet.

Lecture 5.
November 12, 2022

*

The Manifest (*al-Dhahir*)
and the Nonmanifest (*al-Batin*)

Q: A disciple had a dream vision (*ru'ya*) where she saw the Prophet ﷺ and her body disappeared. At the end of the dream, she desired to see the Shaykh instead of the Prophet ﷺ.

Sidi Shaykh first explained that this was previously explained multiple times in terms of direct vision (*mushahada*), not dream vision (*ru'ya*). Ibn al-'Abbas, peace be upon him, reached a state where whenever he looks in the mirror, he sees the image of the Prophet ﷺ instead of his image. This is due to the fact that one cannot witness the Names the Nonmanifest (*al-Batin*) and the Manifest (*al-Dhahir*) at the same time. In the context of visions, when the Name "the Nonmanifest" (*al-Batin*) appears with all of its secrets, the Name "the Manifest" (*al-Dhahir*) must disappear. They can be seen as if the Nonmanifest (*al-Batin*) is the secret of the Manifest (*al-Dhahir*) and vice versa. The same applies to the Names the First (*al-Awwal*) and the Last (*al-Akhir*), one is the secret of the other. They can be brought together in the secret of the Essence, but never in vision. This is evident in the story of Musa, peace be upon him, when he asked his Lord to see Him: "**My Lord! Reveal Yourself to me so I may see You.**" Allah's response was clear: "**You cannot see Me!**"[14]. Even when Allah manifested Himself to the mountain, it disappeared.

This stays valid if projected to creatures. The Prophet ﷺ represents the Light, the reality, and the disciple represents an illusion. Thus, his image cannot coexist with the Prophet's ﷺ image. Even the companions did not coexist with his image, they just coexisted with his Messengerhood (*risala*). If he ﷺ, manifested himself with his reality, they would certainly disappear.

Sidi Shaykh added that seeing the Prophet ﷺ or the Shaykh is the same thing as they both have the same reality. This is evident in the Hadith of Sayyiduna Ali, peace be upon him, when the Prophet ﷺ said to him: "Your Light is from My Light and My Light is from Your Light."[15]

....

14   Quran 7:143.
15   Al-Jouini, Ibrahim. *Fara'id al-Simtayin*. Vol. 1, page 40.

Lecture 6.
November 26, 2022

*

The significance of symbols in the vision of Light

Q: A disciple had a direct vision of Light where she witnessed a sand clock and a six-pointed star.

Sidi Shaykh stated that a sand clock is similar to an 'X' or two opposed triangles. It is a representation of the universe. A triangle represents the numbered Basmala (*al-basmala bil marqum*). The lower triangle in the sand clock is the shadow of the real Basmala represented by the upper triangle. The real Basmala is huge to the point that it cannot be realized. It cannot be pronounced in a few seconds like other words.

Sidi Shaykh said that the six-pointed star represents the six days during which Allah created the universe, with its center representing the Day of Increase (*yawm al-mazid*), which is Friday. When divided into segments it gives twelve, which represent the twelve months.

Sidi Shaykh added that the universe has a movement. Is it a six-pointed star, an 'X', an octagonal star, a circle, or a triangle? Maybe it is moving and changing of form.

The octagonal star, for instance, is a square in a square, four by four, symbolizing "Muhammad x Ahmad". It represents the seven earths, seven heavens, the Footstool, and the Throne. It is the closest to wayfaring (*suluk*) in the Tariqa Karkariya, which is why it is used as the emblem of the Tariqa, with the Arabic word "*al-karkariya*" inscribed at its center.

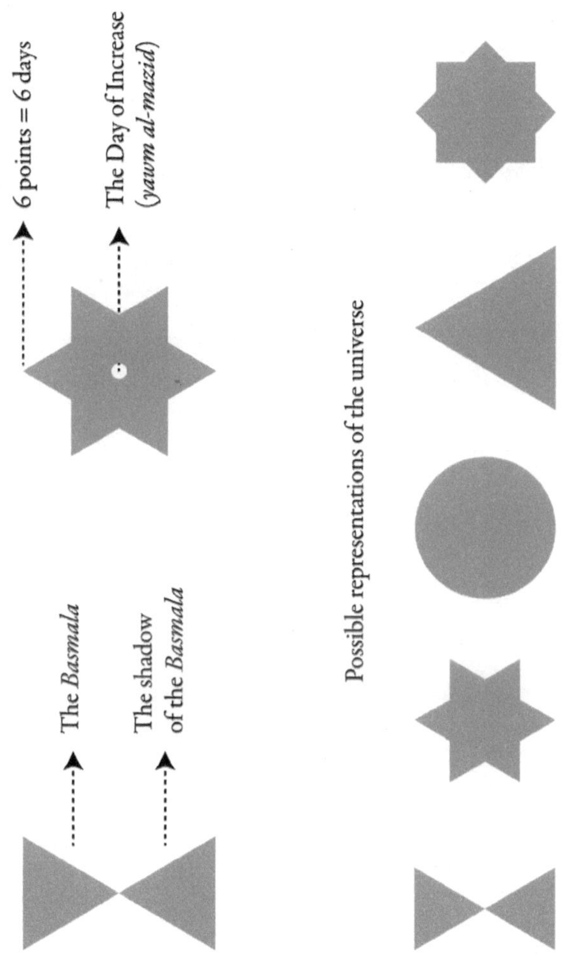

6 points = 6 days
The Day of Increase (yawm al-mazid)
The Basmala
The shadow of the Basmala
Possible representations of the universe

Lecture 7.
December 3, 2022

*

Seeing the Karkariya Shaykh in dream visions

Q: A disciple had two dream visions. In one, he entered a lamp and saw the Light in all directions. In the second, Sidi Shaykh said to him: "I am satisfied with you."

Sidi Shaykh explained that swimming in the Light is how the disciple should be in sleep and wakefulness, he should see nothing but the Light of Allah. This dream vision is a sign for the disciple to work harder to transform the dream into a vision in the state of wakefulness and to extinguish himself in the Light of Allah.

Concerning the second dream, Sidi Shaykh referred to the Hadith of the Prophet ﷺ: "Whoever has seen me in a dream, then no doubt, he has seen me"[16]. This applies to the *Wali*. As long as he didn't say something incomprehensible but rather said that he is satisfied with the disciple, it

....

16   *Sahih Bukhari* #6994.

51

means that he truly is satisfied. Sidi Shaykh then conveyed to the disciple that he loves him for his humility and his recognition that everything comes from Allah and that he possesses nothing himself. Sidi Shaykh referred to the saying of Shaykh al-'Alawi, God have mercy on him: "Neither is for me nor with me".

*

Being entirely for the sake of Allah (*lillah*)

Q: A disciple asked about verse 136 of Surah al-An'am: "And they dedicate to God a share of the crops and cattle He created, saying: "This belongs to God"—or so they claim— "and this belongs to our partners." But that which is for their partners does not reach God, and that which is for God does reach their partners. Evil indeed is the judgment they make!"[17]

In his response, Sidi Shaykh said that what is for God lasts and remains, and what is for other than Him is severed and perishes. Sidi Shaykh gave the example of someone who does not fulfill his obligations such as giving zakat, yet donates money as *sadaqah*. He explained that this does not make sense, and is completely wrong. Fulfilling what's due to Allah should come before thinking about others.

....

17   Quran 6:136.

Sidi Shaykh added that if this approach were to be applied to the disciple, then he should initially fulfill his obligations. His entire journey (*suluk*) should be to Allah (*lillah*), the servant with all that he owns should be to Allah. While normal people engage in *sadaqah*, zakat, obligatory acts, and voluntary deeds, the disciple should be wholly devoted to Allah (*lillah*).

Sidi Shaykh referred to the story of Sayyiduna Abu Bakr, God be pleased with him, when he brought his entire wealth to the Prophet Muhammad ﷺ. When the Prophet ﷺ asked him: "What have you left for your family?" Abu Bakr replied: "I have left Allah and His Messenger for them."[18]

....

18 *Jami' al-Tirmidhi* #3675.

Lecture 8.
December 5, 2022

*

Ahl al-Suffah

Q: A disciple asked about the difference between the companions of Suffah, known as Ahl al-Suffah, and the ten companions to whom paradise was promised.

Sidi Shaykh explained that the companions were chosen by Allah to be in the company of the Prophet ﷺ during his lifetime. Ten among them were specifically chosen to be blessed with paradise in their lives, which is the paradise of knowledge (*jannat al-ma'rifa*) and science. They received the ten lectures of the Name "Allah". Each one had a lecture (*qira'a*). It could be said that they attained spiritual stations (*maqamat*). These companions were always close to the Prophet ﷺ, even their houses were near the mosque of the Prophet ﷺ.

On the other hand, Ahl al-Suffah were also companions of the Prophet ﷺ. The difference is that they were servants in the mosque of the Prophet ﷺ. They resided in a corner (*zawiya*) situated at the rear of the mosque. The concept of "Zawiya" in Sufism originated from this setting. This corner was the original *mihrab* of the mosque of the Prophet ﷺ when Jerusalem (*al-quds*) was the *qibla*. Their area remains known until today within the mosque of the Prophet ﷺ. They detached themselves from worldly possessions, such as homes, spouses, or wealth. Their aim wasn't knowledge or status, but seeking the Face of Allah.

The Prophet ﷺ would stay with them, providing them with food and clothes, they were given precedence in receiving *sadaqah*. They also used to wear colorful clothes resembling the patched cloak. Sidi Shaykh added that some suggest that the term Sufism (*suffiyyah*) derives from their name, Ahl al-Suffah.

Later in the lecture, Sidi Shaykh spoke about people who lived before the Prophet ﷺ. He explained that they should be considered as monotheists (*muwahidin*). However, those who came after Islam should be assessed based on their claimed beliefs. Sidi Shaykh mentioned 'Abdullah Ibn 'Abd al-Mutalib, the father of the Prophet ﷺ. He passed away before the revelation of the Message (*al-risala*) to the Prophet ﷺ, and is considered a monotheist (*muwahhid*).

As for aba lahab, the uncle of the Prophet ﷺ, he died after the revelation of the Prophet's message and did not believe in Allah. Thus, he is considered a polytheist (*mushrik*).

Sidi Shaykh also spoke about Ummuna Amina, the mother of the Prophet ﷺ. When she gave birth to the Prophet ﷺ, she saw the Light coming out of her. She is considered to be among the people of the station of excellence (*maqam al-ihsan*).

Lecture 9.
December 6, 2022

*

The five-pointed star

Q: A disciple asked Sidi Shaykh about the significance of the five-pointed star and whether it represents *Ahl al-Bayt* of the Prophet ﷺ.

Sidi Shaykh responded that, indeed, the five-pointed star represents the Family of the Prophet ﷺ, specifically the People of the Cloak (*ahl al-kisa*) comprising: Sayyiduna al-Hassan, Sayyiduna al-Hussain, Ummuna Fatima al-Zahra, Sayyiduna Ali, and the Prophet ﷺ. In the past people used to represent them with a hand with five fingers and the Name "Allah" written in the center of the hand. This symbol symbolizes the saying of Allah: **"The Hand of God is over their hands."**[19]

Sidi Shaykh added that nowadays, the five-pointed star is used by some other cultures as a symbol of satanism. Speaking about it might lead to accusations of worshiping satan.

....

19   Quran 48:10.

Sidi Shaykh explained that the six-pointed star represents the symbol of the universe (*al-kawn*). It is also associated with the six articles of faith, which include belief in the existence and oneness of Allah, His Angels, His Divine revelations, His Prophets, the Day of Judgement, and the Pre-measurement.

The five-pointed star also symbolizes the five pillars of Islam, which are the profession of faith (*al-shahada*), prayer (*al-salat*), alms (*al-zakat*), fasting (*al-sawm*) in Ramadan, and pilgrimage (*al-hajj*). Their sum equals eleven, which is the number of times Surah al-Ikhlas is recited on the dead person.

*

Facing denial is a *Sunnah*

Q: A disciple dreamt of Sidi Shaykh and other disciples visiting his childhood house. During the gathering, they performed the sacred dance (*al-hadra*). Afterward, when the disciple's family brought food, they forgot to include Sidi Shaykh's meal.

Sidi Shaykh stated that people who are connected to family and friends may face some troubles because of their relationship with the Shaykh. If one follows another person talking in general subjects of religion or any other tariqa, no one will blame him because everyone knows that he will leave it sooner or later. However, when it comes to following the Tariqa Karkariya, it is considered the greatest disaster in the universe, whether family members are Sufi or not, and whether they know the Tariqa or not. Even if one tries to explain they will refuse to hear from him.

This is the *Sunnah* of Prophets, peace be upon them, they were denied by their family members. Sidi Shaykh cited some examples such as Sayyiduna Nuh, peace be upon him, whose child was his biggest enemy. The same with Sayyiduna Ibrahim, peace be upon him, and his uncle who was like a father to him. Sayyiduna Hud, peace be upon him, was also denied by his wife. Also, there is the story of Qabil and Habil, the sons of Sayyiduna Adam, peace be upon them.

Sidi Shaykh said that if the disciple seeks Allah and wants to follow his Shaykh, he should not expect to be accepted by everyone. He should experience an aspect of Prophethood (*nubuwa*). Allah tests the disciple in this regard. If the disciple fears trouble with family because of the Tariqa, he is free to leave the Tariqa and deny the Shaykh, no one is forced to stay. Those who chose the path of Allah over everything, no one told them to do so, it is something natural for them, it is like they were built for it.

Sidi Shaykh explained that it is useless to approach the Shaykh complaining about family members fighting against the disciple due to his association with the Tariqa. He further mentioned that he does not discuss with disciples about those who denied him, instead, he talks only about Allah's Light. Therefore, if one seeks to satisfy his wife, he may consider her as a Shaykh or even a God and prostrate for her. Men do not give up on their principles because of others, all the while maintaining positive family relationships.

Sidi Shaykh added that one should understand that only those who possess the secret of Allah's Light will truly support him in following this Light. What the disciple wears from rosary (*subha*) and patched cloak (*muraqa'a*) are not accessories, these are foundations of the path of Allah. Thus, if one wants to be the Shaykh's disciple he must accept them.

There may come a day when the Shaykh tests the disciple in this, perhaps by visiting him at his workplace and declaring himself as the disciple's father. If the disciple denies his father, it is over for him. Sidi Shaykh added that no one got fired from work because of the Tariqa except for one person, and that is the Shaykh. If a disciple gets fired from his job, he should realize that it was because performing properly, not because of the Tariqa.

*

Salat al-Istiwa'

Q: A disciple asked about *Salat al-Istiwa'* which is a prayer upon the Prophet ﷺ mentioned in the Book of Sidi Shaykh *"al-Ma'arij al-Nuraniyyah fi al-Adhkar al-Karkariya"*.

Sidi Shaykh explained that in this prayer, he cited three of his Shaykhs and ancestors which are Moulay al-Hassan al-Karkari, Moulay al-Taher al-Karkari and Sidi Ibn Kadour al-Boukili. These three Shaykhs have direct family links to Sidi Shaykh. They appear in the five recent tiers of his spiritual and parental chains. The following diagram demonstrates the relationship between Sidi Shaykh and his previously mentioned ancestors.

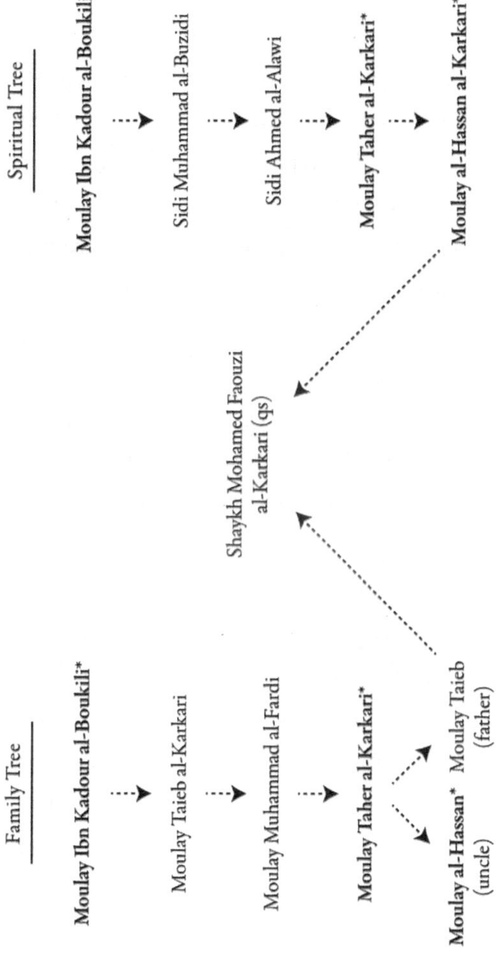

In this prayer called *Salat al-Istiwa'* Sidi Shaykh says: "*Salaat istiwa' min maratib mi'raj, al-Ka'bah al-Quduriyyah wa al-Samawat al-tibaq al-Tahiriyyah wa Sidrat al-Muntaha al-Hasaniyyah.*"

Sidi Shaykh explained, in his response to the disciple's question, that when one talks about Sainthood (*wilaya*), one is not talking about the person but about Sainthood itself. Sidi Ibn Qadur al-Boukili was very famous in his time, drawing visitors from every corner. He was referred to as "*al-Ka'aba al-Quduriyyah*" in *Salat al-Istiwa'*. He was as apparent and recognized in his time as the Kaaba itself.

In contrast, Moulay al-Taher al-Karkari remained concealed during his era. This was due to receiving Shaykhhood (*mashyakha*) during the lifetime of his Shaykh Sidi Ahmad al-'Alawi. In the last years of Sidi al-'Alawi, Moulay al-Taher aided his Shaykh, even in facilitating the entry of disciples into spiritual seclusion. When a disciple was ready for *kholwa*, Sidi al-'Alawi postponed it until Moulay Taher's visit from Morocco to Mustghanem, Algeria. Thus, Moulay al-Taher remained hidden like the heavens. He revealed himself only to people from his town. He was referred to in *Salat al-Istiwa'* as "*al-Samawat al-tibaq al-Tahiriyyah*".

Moulay al-Hassan al-Karkari, the uncle of Sidi Shaykh and his Shaykh, kept his Wilaya hidden. He spoke about it, yet no one comprehended him, and his true nature remained unknown, much like *Sidrat al-Muntaha*. In *Salat al-Istiwa'*, he was referred to as "*Sidrat al-Muntaha al-Hassaniyyah*".

*

Harut and marut

Q: A disciple asked about the reality of harut and marut.

Sidi Shaykh explained that harut and marut are two angels, who, upon coming to the earth fell in the sins of their appetitive and sexual desires.

Sidi Shaykh added that the sin of Sayyiduna Adam, peace be upon him, was eating from the tree. It is the same for harut and marut, they ate but not only this, they fell into fornication with a woman who lured them. At first, they had knowledge and secrets, it was not about magic. They were teaching this knowledge to people until a woman lured them into using this knowledge in illicit ways for personal profit. They imparted these secrets to this woman until the secrets were transformed into magic. They were then offered to choose between hell and prison for what they did and they chose to be in prison.

Sidi Shaykh pointed out that what many people are unaware of is that they are imprisoned on earth. Humans don't know about them, and reciprocally, they don't know about humans. Sidi Shaykh added that maybe there are other things on earth that people don't know about.

*

The trees of *Ahl al-Bayt*

Q: The trees of *Ahl al-Bayt*.

Later in this lecture, Sidi Shaykh spoke about *Ahl al-Bayt*. He said that the Blessed Tree represents *Ahl al-Bayt* of the Prophet ﷺ. He referred to the first verse of Surah al-Tin: **"By the fig and the Olive"**[20]. He explained that the fig tree is also considered a blessed tree. There are two types of *Ahl al-Bayt*: those who are from the olive tree, possess a kernel similar to an olive. They embody both esoteric knowledge (*haqiqa*) and exoteric knowledge (*shari'a*). The others originate from the fig tree, lacking a kernel, embodying only esoteric knowledge (*haqiqa*), and are referred to as "the attracted by the Divine presence of *Ahl al-Bayt*" (*majadhib ahl al-bayt*). The priority is for the olive because it unites both *haqiqa* and *shari'a*.

Sidi Shaykh added that all the trees that Allah positively mentions in the Quran are considered blessed and represent *Ahl al-Bayt*. On the contrary, trees like zaqqum, for example, which are not blessed, represent enemies and individuals who deny *Ahl al-Bayt*. These trees symbolize darkness.

Sidi Shaykh said that the entire earth, encompassing its water and land, is considered a mosque for the Prophet ﷺ. He is the only one to really pray. Other people's prayers

. . . .

20   Quran 95:1.

aren't really prayers compared to his prayers. Sidi Shaykh referred to a part of verse 105 from Surah al-An'am: **"That the earth shall be inherited by My righteous servants."**[21] Sidi Shaykh explained that the righteous servants are *Ahl al-Bayt*. That's why whoever doesn't pray upon them his prayer is not accepted.

*

Eating from the Blessed Tree

Q: In the same context, a disciple asked about the Blessed Tree from which Sayyiduna Adam has eaten.

Sidi Shaykh explained that the sin of Sayyiduna Adam, peace be upon him, is eating from the Blessed Tree. It wasn't the act of eating per se, but mistreating the Blessed Tree led to his descent from paradise to earth. Eating from the Blessed Tree is like taking wealth from orphans. Sidi Shaykh referred to the verse: **"Allah was pleased with the believers when they swore allegiance to you under the tree."**[22] In this verse, Allah didn't mention eating from the Tree but rather sitting beneath it. Even if something falls from the Blessed Tree, eating it is strictly forbidden. This tree is not for eating, this is why one should know how to treat *Ahl al-Bayt* and should never take something from them. Doing

....

21 Quran 6:105.
22 Quran 48:18.

so is like eating from the Blessed Tree. It is preferable to give to them rather than take from them.

Iblis wasn't lying when he described the tree to Sayyiduna Adam, peace be upon him, as a tree of immortality (*al-khuld*) and a kingdom that would never decay. His seduction led Sayyiduna Adam, peace be upon him, to eat from the Tree, which resulted in trouble. However, the description of the Tree's attributes was accurate.

Sidi Shaykh added that this is precisely why it is advisable for disciples to avoid talking about the Shaykh. They can exchange information on performing *dhikr*, understanding the Divine Light's example, and the Zawiya's program and its activities. However, when the discussion centers on the Shaykh it is a red flag. Additionally, some other disciples want to manage and lead without possessing either the rightful authority or the capabilities to do so.

Allah, Prestigious and Majestic, instructed Adam peace be upon him, that he had access to all of paradise for his desires, except for this Tree. Similarly, it applies to the disciple's relationship with the Blessed Tree. The Shaykh represents Allah's Vicegerent on earth, hence, acting in this way is like eating from the Name "Allah"; from the 'Ha' or the '*Lam*', etc. Sidi Shaykh added that one should not talk about the Name "Allah", it is better to keep the chosen by Allah to do so. As for the example of Allah's Light, if one talks about it, he should always refer to the Shaykh because

Allah says: **"Lit from a Blessed Tree"**[23]. So, one should mention the source of his knowledge when he talks.

Sidi Shaykh finished this part by giving the example of people who explain the process in which the Shaykh transmits the Divine Light to the disciple in the pledge of allegiance. He said that regardless of who this individual is, he cannot talk about this and he does not know about it. Talking about things like this is like giving direction to the Tree while it is neither of the east nor the west.

---

23 Quran 24:35.

Lecture 10.
December 12, 2022

*

The shape of the heavens

Q: A disciple had a dream vision in which he witnessed the heaven extending vertically like a wall. There was a door at the bottom from where he crossed from one side to the other.

Sidi Shaykh explained that heaven has both length and width, so it can resemble the one described in this dream. He referred to verse 133 of Surah Al 'Imran: "**and a Garden, the width whereof is as the width of heaven and earth.**"[24] And the Hadith of the Prophet ﷺ: "The first heaven compared to the second heaven, is like a small ring thrown into a desert. The second heaven compared to the third heaven, is like a small ring thrown into a desert [...] The seventh heaven compared to the Footstool (*kursi*) ring is like a small ring

....

24 Quran 3:133.

69

thrown into a desert, and the Footstool compared to the Throne (*'arsh*) is like a small ring thrown into a desert."[25]

Sidi Shaykh stated that Sayyiduna Ali, may Allah honor his face, said that the heavens are in the form of a horn. If one pictures those rings, one on top of another, where the upper ring is the largest and the lower ring is the smallest, the rings will form a 'V' shape. Sayyiduna Ali, may Allah honor his face, also mentioned that the Earth is like a grain on a bull's horn. This horn is upside down, with the smallest end at the bottom and the largest end at the top.

Sidi Shaykh added that the Prophet ﷺ described the width of the bridge (*al-sirat*) as thinner than a hair and sharper than a sword. This width represents what one has done in his life, while the length is fixed. The first group to cross the bridge have faces that are like the moon. They pass swiftly like lightning over the bridge. Then the second group, their faces are brighter than the most resplendent star in the sky. For them, the bridge has no width, only length. This is what is described as the straight path (*al-sirat al-mustaqim*) in Surah al-Fatiha.

Sidi Shaykh added that people always work on the width but forget about the length which is the most important. All of the objects and material things that one carries burden him in the width. If one is only attached to Allah, the bridge will be thinner than a hair and sharper than a sword as described by the Prophet ﷺ. In the spiritual seclusion

....

25   Al-Alussi, Muhammad. *Ruh al-Ma'ani Fi Tafsir al-Sab'u al-Mathani.*

(*kholwa*), the Shaykh works on the lengthy with the disciple when he asks him to gather the rings which are the heavens. He also asks him to not search for what is inside the rings. Searching for what exists in every ring represents working on the width, whereas the Shaykh wants the disciple to work on the length.

Sidi Shaykh returned to the last part of the dream when the disciple crossed the door from one side to the other. He explained that according to Sayyiduna Ali, may Allah honor his face: "The earth is like a grain on a bull's horn" signifying that the end of the heavens is the earth. The disciple's place is not here on earth but up in the heavens. Therefore, one should strive to attain this elevated station if he claims to be a member of the Prophet's ﷺ community (*ummah*).

*

The significance of dots in Arabic letters

Q: A disciple had a direct vision (*mushahada*) of Light in which he witnessed three stars.

Sidi Shaykh first stated that when one talks about the secret of letters or the science of letters, it is, in fact, the Dot (*al-nuqta*) itself. Sidi Shaykh referred to the saying of Sayyiduna Ali, may Allah honor his face: "The secret of the letter 'Ba' is the Dot". The Dot is unique, and to claim to possess the Dot, one should have the twenty-one Divine secrets of the Dot called *al-musalamat.* This is when one can distinguish between the origin and the branch. While the branch can return to the origin, the origin never returns to the branch.

[Note: *al-musalamat* are the Divine secrets of the Dot in the Name of Majesty "Allah".]

Sidi Shaykh further explained that the origin of the letter *'Ba'* is the Dot, not the letter *'Ba'* itself. The presence of multiple dots in the direct vision of Light indicates that one is working on the reflection of the Dot. In the Basmala, there are three dots that can also be considered four due to the split of the dot of the letter 'Ya' in al-Rahim.

Sidi Shaykh added that Sayyiduna Ali, may Allah honor his face, was the one who introduced dots in the Quran. Before that, it consisted only of letters. He placed a dot for the letter *'Ba'* under the line or beneath the central part of the letter, making it a dot from the realm of invincibility (*nuqta jabarutiyyah*). As for the letter 'Nun', he placed the dot on top of the letter, making it a dot from the spiritual realm (*nuqta malakutiyyah*). Similarly, the dot of the letter 'Jim' is also from the realm of invincibility as it was positioned under the line.

Letters are between the spiritual realm and the realm of invincibility as if the science of the Dot doesn't exist in the physical realm (*al-mulk*). When Sayyiduna Ali, may Allah honor his face, wanted to give it a shape, he created it in the form of the *hamza* at the end of the word as in the word water (*ma'*). The *hamza*, written on the line, resembles a dot. It is regarded as a dot and can be substituted with a dot when written.

Sidi Shaykh added that an Arabic letter can be divided into three parts: one from the realm of invincibility, one from the spiritual realm, and one from the physical realm. For example, in the case of the letter 'Jim', the portion above the line pertains to the spiritual realm, the portion on the line corresponds to the physical realm, and the portion below the line belongs to the realm of invincibility.

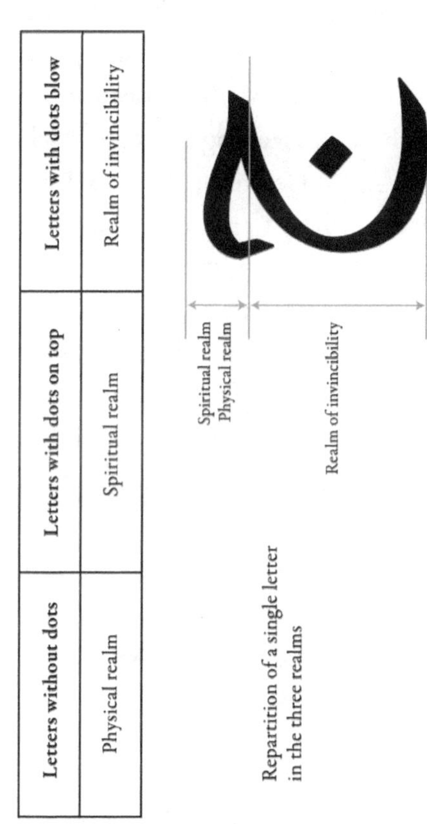

Sidi Shaykh added that in Arabic, there are twenty-one dots and twenty-eight letters. Their sum totals thirty-nine, and with the secret of comprehension, they reach forty, corresponding to the soul that completed the forty degrees (*al-nafs al-arba'iniyyah*).

Sidi Shaykh also stated that the Arabic language is a living language and that the number of dots in the Arabic letters corresponds to the number of lectures in the Dot of the Name of Majesty "Allah". It is impossible to read these twenty-one lectures before finishing the lectures of the letters of the Name "Allah", as one cannot read the secret of the spirit before reading the secret of the body. In other words, one should learn the shape and the arc of the letter and then know how to put dots and why there are dots in one letter and not in another.

Sidi Shaykh stated that the dot of the letter '*Ba*' is the dot of Sayyiduna Ali, may Allah honor his face, the dot of the letter 'Nun' is of Ummuna Fatima al-Zahra, and the dots of the letter 'Ya' are of Sayyiduna al-Hassan and Sayyiduna al-Hussain, peace be upon them. This 'Ya' represents the ten lectures.

Sidi Shaykh also spoke about *qawasim al-Quran*. He stated that these letters represent *Ahl al-Bayt*, peace be upon them. He added that this is unreachable with the intellect; as it is an experiential science. By following *Ahl al-Bayt* who possess this science, one can reach closeness to God. Otherwise, there is no such closeness.

Sidi Shaykh added that the knowledge of Sayyiduna Ali, may Allah honor his face, was hidden in the realm of invincibility until he married Ummuna Fatima al-Zahra, peace be upon her. It then transitioned into the spiritual realm, akin to the 'Nun' of Ummuna Fatima al-Zahra. When Sayyiduna al-Hassan and Sayyiduna al-Hussain, peace be upon them, were born, this knowledge was revealed and became apparent on earth.

These four dots of the People of the Cloak (*ahl al-kisa*) are gathered around the Ahmadian *Alif* (*al-alif al-ahmadi*). From there, the Names are split: the First, the Last, the Manifest, and the Nonmanifest. The four dots surrounding the Ahmadian *Alif* form the tree, with each dot representing an olive. One who reaches the shadow of the tree vanishes from the east and the west, signifying the absence of width and the attainment of closeness to Allah. Such a person journeys along the *Alif* until becoming a line. This is what is meant by the verse of Surah al-Fatiha: "**Guide us to the straight path**"[26]. The next verse in the same Surah: "**the path of those You have blessed**"[27], refers to those whom Allah has indeed blessed, the *Ahl al-Bayt* of the Prophet ﷺ.

....

26   Quran 1:6.
27   Quran 1:7.

Lecture 11.
December 12, 2022

*

Witnessing the Light in objects

Q: In a direct vision of Light (*mushahada*), a disciple witnessed the Light entering and leaving his body.

Sidi Shaykh explained that by saying that the Light is in the disciple's heart, it is not meant in the heart as an organ, but rather in his inner (*batin*). The Light does not have an exact location but flows throughout the entire body, much like the breath. If the Light disappears from the body, the body becomes inanimate and useless because this body is alive with the Light that Allah has placed within it. This Light is revealed to those chosen by Allah, but cannot be seen as it is. Thus, Allah gave the example of this Light in the form of a niche, a lamp, a crystal, and a shining star. If Allah were to lift all the veils between Himself and humans, revealing the reality of the Divine Light, all humans would vanish and decay.

Sidi Shaykh added that there is no existence alongside the Divine Light. Allah has created all creatures with His Light, it is not adequate to say that the Light exists in some creatures and not in others. Allah has lifted the veil for some of His creatures so they can witness the Light and understand the relationship between the Creator and the created. These individuals are known as the people of the elite (*ahl al-khasa*).

Sidi Shaykh added that claiming one's existence implies a form of association (*shirk*) as it suggests co-existence with the Creator. The perception of oneself and surrounding objects stems from one's distance from Allah. If one is close to Allah, he will see nothing but Him. When Allah reveals this reality, He shows His servant this Light based on his presence and readiness. Consequently, the servant perceives this Light within himself and in the objects around him. For example, during prayer, he may see it in the prayer carpet, and outdoors, he may see it in rocks, until he comprehends that all these objects are like a mirage. It is not strange to see the Light in objects, but what is really strange is to see the object and not the Light.

When one reaches this state, it is as if he has a double vision. An enlightened vision with which one sees the pure meanings (*al-ma'ani*), and a vision of darkness with which he sees receptacles (*al-awani*). This mixed scene will depend on one's closeness to Allah.

Sidi Shaykh further explained that disciples may think that these objects are shining Light. For example, when one witnesses a vase surrounded by Light, he says that this vase is enlightened, but when he sees a tree not surrounded by Light, he says this tree is not enlightened. In reality, it is just the disciple's presence with Allah that varies from one scene to another.

Sidi Shaykh projected this explanation onto the disciple's dream. He stated that the body is a creation of Allah. If one looks at his body with a presence with Allah, he will witness the Light flowing through the body, the same as he sees the Light flowing in objects. It depends on one's starting point, whether it is himself or the horizons.

Sidi Shaykh added that the first step is to close the eyes, turn off the light, detach oneself from images and objects, and practice remembrance (*dhikr*) of Allah. Some claim that images are prohibited in places of prayer. They forget that they themselves are images, and their pockets often contain money adorned with pictures. In fact, the images should be removed from the heart, not from the house. Allah says: **"Neither my earth nor my heaven sufficed me, but the heart of my faithful servant sufficed me."**[28] Thus, the faithful servant has no images in his heart, he has only Allah.

Sidi Shaykh referenced the beginning of verse 35 of Surah al-Nur: **"God is Light"**[29]. To give an example of this Divine Attribute to His servants, Allah mentioned the example of His Light in the Quran. This example can be seen in all objects and creatures but the closest is to see it from where one has taken this example of Light which is the Shaykh.

....

28 Ibn ʿArabi, Muhyi al-Din. *Al-Futuhat al-Makiyyah*. Vol. 1, Page 216.
29 Quran 24:35.

It is easier and faster to see the Light when one is with his Shaykh than when he is looking at objects and trees. He can consider the Shaykh as the gate to the unseen (*al-ghayb*).

Sidi Shaykh added that the Prophet ﷺ is the Luminous Lamp (*al-siraj al-munir*). His reality, which is Light, can be seen in everything, but the closest is in *Ahl al-Bayt* and the Quran, the book of Allah. If one doesn't have a relationship with the Shaykh, even if he sees the Light he cannot interpret it and understand its language. It is evident in the story of Sayyiduna Musa, peace be upon him, and Sayyiduna al-Khidr, peace be upon him. Academic studies and background won't help in this matter. One needs the gate to the spiritual realm (*al-malakut*), he needs the One who has the keys. The further the disciple is from the Shaykh, the more he is in darkness. If his absence is long, he will start to have doubts about the Light and will try to understand it with his limited intellect.

Sidi Shaykh added that even in the books of the folk of Allah (*ahl Allah*), they direct the reader to seek out a Shaykh. Once found, it is from the Shaykh that knowledge is acquired, not from books. So, when someone says that he sees the Light coming out of him, it is as if he is attributing it to himself. To avoid falling into something that distances him from the presence of Allah, one needs one thing: to acknowledge and believe that this Light he got is from the Shaykh. This is a reality.

When one came to pledge allegiance to the Shaykh, Allah placed this Light in his heart, and through the Shaykh, he received his share (*qisma*). One shouldn't think that he owns this Light. The Light is not an object to be owned. Allah says in the Quran: "**God is the Light of the heavens and the earth**"[30]. Thus, one has no right to claim ownership of the Light or say it is his own. This Light is an unveiling, a subtle flow (*sarayan*), a connection. As for darkness, it is the opposite, it is a separation.

One shouldn't think that satan (*iblis*) will come to him and push him to commit a sin or a major sin. Instead, satan will enter into him through the door of lying, pushing him not to recognize the Light and the Divine secret. That's why when the Prophet ﷺ was asked if a faithful servant could fall into fornication, he replied that the faithful servant does not lie. It means that maybe he falls into fornication, but when asked about it, he doesn't lie, he admits it. That's the main characteristic of a Muslim, honesty. So, when one recognizes the Divine Light, he becomes honest.

Sidi Shaykh added that when one enters the Tariqa, he receives permission (*idhn*) for remembrance (*dhikr*), permission for the pledge of allegiance (*bay'ah*), permission for the spiritual seclusion (*kholwa*), etc. Therefore, he should refrain from talking in matters for which he lacks permission, as doing so may lead to distancing himself from the presence (*al-hadra*), especially if he relies on his own intelligence to

....

30 Quran 24:35.

get secrets, etc. Sidi Shaykh referenced the saying: "Stay in the station where Allah has placed you". So, one better avoid searching into other areas, as doing so may exhaust him. If he persists, he may stray from the Tariqa, not only rejecting the Shaykh but also the Sufi Masters and the folk of Allah (*ahl Allah*).

Lecture 12.
December 18, 2022

*

How to deal with the soul (*al-nafs*)

Q: A disciple asked Sidi Shaykh how one should love his soul (*nafs*) and not hate it.

Sidi Shaykh started his response by stating that Allah created seven levels (*maratib*) for the soul. The following figure details the seven of them.

The levels of the soul (*maraitb al-nafs*)

The perfect soul (*al-kamila*)

The pleasing soul (*al-mardiyya*)

The pleased soul (*al-radhiyya*)

The tranquil soul (*al-muttma'ina*) --------► The isthmus (*al-barazakh*)

The inspired soul (*al-mulhama*)

The blaming soul (*al-lawwama*)

The commanding soul (*al-ammara*)

*"Contradict it
but don't hate it"*
Shaykh Ahmed al-Alawi

Sidi Shaykh explained that the tranquil soul represents the isthmus (*al-barzakh*). He referenced the verse: "**O tranquil soul! Return to your Lord, well pleased and well pleasing.**"[31] It is as if this soul is the gate to return to Allah.

If the soul is tranquil with Allah and feels secure with His Divine Names and Divine Attributes, then one should not hate it but rather accompany it. However, in the beginning, one should contradict it. This is not because the soul is an enemy but rather because one has yet to realize its secret. The soul represents a steed (*buraq*) sent by Allah to the servant to use it to return to Him. One thinks of the soul as an enemy that influenced him and kept him away from Allah, and from this soul, he acquired pride (*kibr*), wonder (*'ujub*), etc. It is absurd to consider as an enemy the very means and the tool that will bring one to know his Lord.

Sidi Shaykh added that one should initially contradict the soul (*al-nafs*), not because it is his enemy, but because he does not understand its allusions and the it conveys. He should therefore teach it humility, for it is through the two opposites the Divine secret is known. When the soul instills arrogance, one counters it with humility, when it instills Lordship, one counters it with servanthood. This is how one begins his journey of wayfaring (*suluk*) and continues it until the soul lifts the veil and reveals its secrets to him. Thus, he discovers that his soul is the perfect means to know Allah. This is why one cannot perceive it as his enemy because the soul itself is the spirit (*al-ruh*), and the soul is

....

31 Quran 89:27-28.

the secret, the secret of secrets, the secret of the Essence, and the secret of Attributes and Names of Allah. Some people have separated the soul from the spirit because they don't understand its secret. Thus, they suggest considering it an enemy, attributing to it a lower station (*manzila sufliyyah*).

Sidi Shaykh added that whoever considers his soul as an enemy, will do the same with his brothers. He referenced the Hadith of the Prophet ﷺ: "A believer is the mirror of his brother."[32] He also referred to the verse: "**Certainly, there has come to you a Messenger from among yourselves.**" He explained that this means that the reality of the soul is the Prophet ﷺ. Only Allah can realize this.

Sidi Shaykh added that when the soul becomes a perfect soul it transforms into a spirit. To be more precise the soul becomes a theater or a recipient in which the soul flows. When the soul ascends, it does so only under the direction of the spirit.

The soul tends to guide itself to become a perfect soul, which means a spirit. However, this transformation is impossible without a teacher or guide acting as the mediator (*al-wassita*). This mediator is the Elite of the Family of the Prophet ﷺ (*'itrat ahl al-bayt*) which represents the *qibla* of the spirit to the disciple.

....

32   Al-Bukhari, Muhammad. *Al-Adab al-Mufrad.* #238.

*

Projecting thoughts on the Quran and the *Sunnah*

Q: A disciple stated that from time to time a verse from the Quran comes to his mind.

Sidi Shaykh said that everything one sees is a verse sent from Allah to him. The smallest detail in one's existence is a verse from Allah, and it is up to him to receive the message sent by Allah.

Sidi Shaykh added that when it comes to thoughts, one should always project them on the Quran and *Sunnah*. If the thought conforms to the Quran and the *Sunnah*, it can be applied, otherwise, this thought is either from the soul or from satan.

Sidi Shaykh was about to conclude the lecture with prayers upon the Prophet ﷺ as usual, when he explained an aspect regarding these prayers. He explained that to recognize one's own weakness and reality, when he wishes to send prayers upon the Prophet ﷺ he says: "O Allah send prayers upon Sayyiduna Muhammad". One asks Allah to pray upon the Prophet ﷺ as Allah is the only One to know his reality and value. As for others, they are not apt to pray on him ﷺ. When one prays one time upon the Prophet ﷺ, Allah prays tenfold upon him. This is the greatness of Allah. What's one's position and station so that he deserves the prayer of Allah upon him?

Lecture 13.
December 19, 2022

*

Awakening through the Divine Light

Q: The Prophet ﷺ said: "The people are asleep and only wake when they die."[33]

Sidi Shaykh commented that people are asleep in this world (*dunya*). Some are in a dream state (*hulum*), while others are in a dream vision (*ru'ya*). A dream (*hulum*) comes from the devil to those who do not follow the Prophet's ﷺ law and disbelieve in it. Disbelief (*kufr*) does not mean to deny or to insult the Prophet's ﷺ law, rather simply the fact that one knows the *Sunnah* of the Prophet ﷺ and does not follow it is considered *kufr*.

The *Sunnah* is revealed by the Prophet ﷺ to Muslims to follow it as a law of living in the physical realm (*mulk*). When discussing the *Sunnah*, some might say that it is just a *Sunnah*, not an obligation. It is perceived that when one

....

33   Al-Ghazali, Abu Hamid. *Ihya 'ulum al-din*. Vol.3, Page 24.

follows it, he is rewarded, and when one ignores it, it is not a big deal. The reality is if one ignores the *Sunnah* of the Prophet ﷺ he is just asleep.

On the other hand, by following the *Sunnah*, not only does one receive rewards, but also awakens from heedlessness (*ghafla*). This law sent by Allah to Muslims through the Prophet ﷺ, cannot be shortened to just five prayers a day. It serves as a comprehensive guide for every aspect of life. All actions and interactions should adhere to its principles. The Prophet ﷺ even instructed on matters such as how to sleep, undress, look, talk, move, etc. Every movement, every second has a science (*'ilm*) from the Prophet ﷺ.

Therefore, by following him in all of these acts, one becomes a being from the spiritual realm (*malakut*) living in the physical realm (*mulk*). This *Sunnah* is a revelation, and a revelation comes from the realm of invincibility (*jabarut*) to the spiritual realm to the physical realm. Otherwise, if one's acts and sayings are from the physical realm he becomes dead and useless. One should not imagine that Allah created him to eat, drink, and marry. That's the lowest level of existence.

Allah created humans to worship Him. Sidi Shaykh referred to the verse: "**And I did not create jinn and humans except to worship Me.**"[34] Sayyiduna Ibn al-'Abbas, may Allah be pleased with him, known as the inkpot of the *ummah*, explained the phrase "**To worship Me**" as "To know Me". Even if one worships Allah without knowing Him, it is like blindly imitating acts without knowing their mean-

....

34   Quran 51:56.

ings. When one does an act and knows what he is doing, this creates piety in him. If one follows the Prophet's ﷺ *Sunnah* blindly, that is fine. However, when one seeks to explore and comprehend it, this will prevent the soul and the whispers (*waswas*) from bringing negative thoughts, pushing him into disbelieving the *Sunnah*, as a lot of young people do nowadays.

Sidi Shaykh added that death is an inevitable passage for every human being. However, one can choose a death that is self-elected, known as the chosen death (*al-mawt al-ikhtiari*). If one does not choose death, he will inevitably experience it. However, by choosing it willingly, he will face it with love and longing to meet Allah. Therefore, it is essential for one to self-contemplate and determine whether he loves death or hates it. If he loves death then he is on the path of the Prophet ﷺ. Otherwise, he is in heedlessness. Sidi Shaykh referred to the verse: **"Can those who had been dead, to whom We gave life and a Light with which they can walk among people."**[35] So, if one thinks that he is alive and on the *Sunnah* of the Prophet ﷺ, he should prove it and reveal the Light of the Prophet ﷺ within him.

Sidi Shaykh added that many have abandoned their religion for the sake of the wife, the children, the girlfriend, etc. The problem is that despite knowing their religion and studying it, they accuse anyone discussing with them about their situation of not being up to date with this era.

....

35 Quran 6:122.

Sidi Shaykh added that everything one sees around him are messages from Allah. If one regards them as a steed to ascend to Allah then, he wins. However, if they lead him away from Allah, then these messages are from satan. The problem lies not in the message itself but in the person's perception and whether he perceives it with an enlightened vision or not.

Sidi Shaykh said that some have seen the Light of Allah, some have heard about it, some have denied it, and some have seen it and neglected it. Those who denied and rejected the Light have chosen to remain dead, even when the path is shown to them. The Prophet ﷺ was Light. Abu jahl and abu lahab witnessed him, interacted with him, and acknowledged his honesty, etc. However, they have never seen his Light. They were only preoccupied with business and pursuing their own interest.

It is the same with the Light of Allah. For instance, when one says maybe it is a visual illusion or thinks that by practicing remembrance of Allah all day long for this Light he will lose his business. It is as if he does not do the litany (*al-wird*) or the remembrance he'll become the richest person on earth. One should keep in mind that he will stay the poorest and will fall in shameful deeds because Allah says in the Quran: **"The devil threatens you with poverty and bids you to shameful deeds."**[36] Shameful deeds are a scandal even if one is in his house. They don't happen when one is alone, but rather in public that he will do it.

....

36   Quran 2:268.

Sidi Shaykh added that the other category of people, those who recognize the Light, have come to understand the verse: **"Order your family to pray and be patient in it. We do not ask you for provisions, rather, it is We who provide for you."**[37] They understood that sustenance comes from Allah whether they work or not. One might question: "How can I stay at home, not work, and still have Allah provide sustenance for me?" This is the reality, whether one accepts it or not. Allah has created His servants and their actions.

Sidi Shaykh added that this verse is an order from Allah. He also stated that in addition to ordering his family to pray, one needs to teach them that Allah is the Provider, neither their jobs, studies, nor even their intelligence will provide for them.

After speaking about those who deny and those who recognize the Light of Allah, Sidi Shaykh spoke about another category of people: those who neglect and contempt the Light of Allah. He stated that the Light of Allah is not the light of the sun, the moon, or a lamp in the physical realm (*mulk*). He added that the human being was created from a clot (*'alaqa*), semen, and a humble fluid (*ma' mahin*) and no one has contempt for him. Yet, when he becomes a human being, he argues and expresses his opinions, but he forgets his reality. How could he forget his reality and disregard the Light of Allah? If the sperm that comes from a creature is not disregarded because it will eventually develop into a human being, then shouldn't this human being, who

....

37   Quran 20:132.

disregards the Light of Allah, realize that he is asleep? In fact, he is not asleep, he is dead.

Sidi Shaykh added that it is with the Light of Allah that one wakes up, not with his intelligence. If one is seeking to be alive (*hayy*), he should recognize who is the Living (*al-Hayy*). It is Allah; life is an attribute of Allah. So, if one wants to be alive, he needs the Light of Allah.

Sidi Shaykh finished this part by stating that when one is witnessing the Light of Allah, he is alive, but when he is not, he is dead. Therefore, a person can experience being dead and coming alive multiple times a day.

Later in this lecture, Sidi Shaykh said that in previous years, when a woman left her house, she would be accompanied by a *mahram*, and she would maintain a high level of respect, no one would be able to see any part of her body. [Note: a mahram is a family member with whom marriage would be considered permanently unlawful in Islam, such as a brother or a father.]

Nowadays, when someone sees his sister or daughter with a man who is not a *mahram* in the street, he may not say anything to her because times have changed, and it has become a common behavior for everyone.

Sidi Shaykh also discussed the inventions and cultural influences that Muslims have imported from western culture, which have impacted Muslim behaviors and traditions. He said that shameful deeds (*al-fahcha'*) have spread to every home. For instance, as long as there's Wi-Fi in a house, those deeds are present there too. Then, after falling into such deeds, one says that Allah is Forgiving (*Ghafur*) and Ever-Merciful (*Rahim*). Allah is indeed Forgiving and Ever-Merciful, but this comes along with the servant's acts, as one dies on the acts that he was doing during his life.

Sidi Shaykh returned to speak about people who neglect the Light. He said that one pretends to love the Prophet ﷺ, but let's go of his Light. If one truly loves the Prophet ﷺ, he will adhere to His Light and never leave it, instead of being attached to objects. What one is doing is forgetting about the Light and moving farther away from it through his actions and sins.

Sidi Shaykh further explained that this world does not equal a mosquito's wing for Allah, but His Light, on the other hand, is the source of the creation of the heavens and the earth. If one understands that the Light is the reality of all that he sees, he will be willing to sacrifice everything he owns, from time and money to distractions and every single thing for this Light. Instead, one is sacrificing the Light of Allah for the smallest and lowest atom in the mosquito's wing, not even for the entire wing.

Sidi Shaykh referred to the Hadith of the Prophet ﷺ: "This world is cursed and what is in it is cursed, except the remembrance (*dhikr*) of Allah, or one who has knowledge (*'alim*) or who acquires knowledge (*muta'alim*)."[38]

Commenting on this Hadith, Sidi Shaykh said that one should look at himself and see which category he fits into. If he is from the people of the remembrance of Allah, then he should know that remembrance is Light. If he is a scholar,

....

38 Ibn Majah, Muhammad. *Sunan Ibn Majah*. Vol.1, Page 1377, #4112.

then also knowledge is Light. And if he is seeking knowledge, then he should apply what he has learned, and then Allah will teach him what he doesn't already know. The fruit of knowledge is Light.

Sidi Shaykh finished this part by saying that the Prophet ﷺ, the Luminous Lamp *(al-siraj al-munir)*, is Light. Sidi Shaykh referred to the Hadith: "The first thing that Allah created is the Light of your Prophet, O Jabir."[39] Thus, if one denies the Light he denies the Prophet ﷺ.

Sidi Shaykh stated that one needs to wake up and wash himself with the Light of Allah before they wash him, in reference to the washing of the dead. And shroud himself with the Light of Allah before they shroud him in white. Water and shroud decay but the Light of Allah lasts.

....

39   Al-ʾAjluni, Ismaʿil. *Kachf al-Khafaʾ*. Vol.1, #827.

Lecture 14.
December 21, 2022

*

The relationship between the disciple and the *Wali*

Q: The relationship between the disciple and the *Wali*.

The Prophet ﷺ said: "There are people from the servants of Allah who are neither prophets nor martyrs; the prophets and martyrs will envy them on the Day of Resurrection for their rank from Allah, the Most High." They asked: "Tell us, Messenger of Allah, who are they?" He replied: "They are people who love one another with the Light of Allah, without having any mutual kinship and giving property to one. I swear by Allah, their faces will glow and they will be sitting in pulpits of Light. They will have no fear when the people will have fear, and they will not grieve when the people will grieve." He then recited the following Quranic verse: **"Behold! Verily for the *Awliya'* of Allah there is no fear, nor shall they grieve."**[40]

....

40   Al-Sijistani, Abu Dawud. *Sunan Abi Dawud*. #3527.

97

Sidi Shaykh commented on this Hadith. He said that these people to whom the Prophet ﷺ refers aren't from the same family or the same country. They are not just united together, but they love one another. Sidi Shaykh explained that without love there is neither wayfaring (*suluk*) nor spiritual attraction (*jadhb*), nor benefice. The disciple wins when love reaches his heart, when he loves his Shaykh more than his money, his child, and even himself.

The Prophet ﷺ said: "None of you will have faith till he loves me more than his father, his children and all mankind."[41] Sidi Shaykh said that one might find this strange and ask: "If this saying is from the Prophet ﷺ, then what's its relation with the *Wali*, and why should one love him more than himself?" Sidi Shaykh then referred to the Hadith of the Prophet ﷺ: "I am leaving among you two weighty things: The Book of Allah and the Elite (*'itra*) of my household (*ahl al-bayt*)."[42] And the Quranic verse: **"And know that the Messenger of Allah is among you."**[43]

Sidi Shaykh explained that the Prophet ﷺ has left a clear message to Muslims. He left the Elite (*'itra*) of *Ahl al-Bayt* that one is required to love them more than everything else. This is when one tastes the submission to the secret of Allah.

Sidi Shaykh referenced the Hadith in which Allah says: "O son of Adam, I fell ill and you visited Me not. He will say: O Lord, and how should I visit You when You are the

....

41　*Sahih Bukhari* #15.
42　*Jami' al-Tirmidhi* #3788.
43　Quran 49:7.

Lord of the worlds? He will say: Did you not know that My servant So-and-so had fallen ill and you visited him not?"[44]

Sidi Shaykh explained that this servant is not anyone but the *Wali* of this person's time. If one were to visit him, he would not receive a reward (*ajr*) but would instead find Allah. Simply by visiting the *Wali* when he is sick, one gains knowledge of Allah.

Sidi Shaykh also referenced the Quranic verse: **"We made Solomon to understand it."**[45] He explained that Sayyiduna Sulayman, peace be upon him, understood it when he became *Bismillah al-Rahman al-Rahim*. Allah says in Surah al-Naml: **"It is from Solomon, and it is 'In the Name of Allah—the Most Compassionate, Most Merciful'."**[46]

Sidi Shaykh explained that Sayyiduna Sulayman, peace be upon him, have understood the matter when he became the essence of the Basmala (*'ayn al-basmala*), not by reading books of Sufism and Saints. One understands when he finds the One who guides him, changes him, and reveals to him the secret of the Dot. When Sayyiduna Ali, may Allah honor his face, said: "I am the Dot", it meant "I am the secret of *Bismillah*, I am the essence of *Bismillah*, I am the attributes of *Bismillah*." On the other hand, if someone doesn't know anything about *Bismillah*, even if he claims it, he is far from understanding it.

....

44   *Sahih Muslim* #2569.
45   Quran 21:79.
46   Quran 27:30.

Sidi Shaykh added that the relationship with the *Wali* is entirely beneficial. Some might think that by following the *Wali*, they may lose their money, wives, etc. In reality, if they will lose them while with the *Wali*, they will lose them anyway. However, when losing something with the *Wali*, it will result in elevation and will have something behind it. Additionally, if one gives up on something for the sake of Sainthood (*wilaya*), then Allah will replace him with something more precious, and even if he does not receive a replacement, he will get a reward (*ajr*) that he cannot realize in this world (*dunya*) and in the hereafter (*akhirah*). This is why the reality of wayfaring is surrender (*taslim*). Surrender (*taslim*) and peace (*salam*) are necessary in wayfaring which is why one says: "*al-salat wa salam 'ala ali Rassoul Allah*". This prayer (*salat*) and peace (*salam*) serve to maintain a connection with the *Ahl al-Bayt* of the Prophet ﷺ. In reality, *Ahl al-Bayt* do not require anyone to pray upon them, as Allah and the angels already pray upon them. However, one requires this connection to them so that Allah purifies his heart, and thus his path to Allah becomes faster. This surrender is necessary, but it should not involve pretense as the Shaykh knows the disciple and knows everyone in his era of 100 years, from young to old.

Sidi Shaykh added that people are divided. There are the believers, people who have faith but only on the apparent side as they don't know anything about the Light of faith. Allah sends to them the *Wali*. He will search for them in the area that is predetermined for him. There are Saints sent to a village, they will search for people of faith in this village. Others are sent to a country, they will accept only people from this country, but reject others. And then there are Saints who are sent for everyone on earth. The *Wali* sent for the entire earth is the reason for salvation. He accepts everyone, however he is. He teaches him how to get out of the darkness of the soul to the Light of Allah.

Sidi Shaykh added that some say that they don't witness the Light. This is because they are immersed in their thoughts and whispers, even the litany (*al-wird*) they don't do it. Sidi Shaykh referred to the saying: "He who has no litany (*wird*) has no love (*widd*)". These will always be in stress and darkness. Sidi Shaykh referred to the verse: "**Thus did Our signs come to you, and you forgot them; and thus, will you this Day be forgotten.**"[47]

Sidi Shaykh said that this was some talking about Sainthood (*al-wilaya*), the center of the eternal truth that if it enlightens the vision of lovers, their nights become days and they will never have nights. Allah enlightened their path to taste the closeness to their Lord and to become in a direct junction (*wasl*) with Him and never get distracted from Him.

Sidi Shaykh then continued to the next part of the Hadith that he mentioned earlier: "O son of Adam, I asked you for food and you fed Me not."[48] Sidi Shaykh explained that it is the same with the *Wali*. Since the pledge of allegiance, the disciple's life, business, etc., have been improving. Then

....

47   Quran 20:126.
48   *Sahih Muslim* #2569.

the disciple comes to the *Wali* and tells him about that. The *Wali* will say to him: "*Ma sha' Allah*, Allah is who provides sustenance and goodness, and prevents the bad from happening. Allah has rewarded you for your hard work, etc." The *Wali* attributes this goodness to the disciple and Allah, but how should the disciple act in this case? He should return the blessing (*al-baraka*) to its origin, to its source, otherwise the source will dry up.

Later in the lecture, Sidi Shaykh spoke about the importance of finding a real *Wali*. He said that some spend seventy years in a tariqa and don't get anything. The one they follow cannot even save himself, so how will he save them?

One will ask: "How will I find the one?" The answer is through the prayer of consultation. One should ask Allah and not waste his time. He should ask Allah and the Prophet ﷺ where to find his grandson, his inheritor. The Prophet will certainly ﷺ guide him. He should also ask Allah where to find his treasure, his gate. Once found, one should never give up on him.

Sidi Shaykh asked: "Did the Prophet ﷺ send a sign?" No, because one is seeking reward (*ajr*), not love. Those who seek rewards will obtain them, but the concern is that they might continue to work for rewards in this life and the hereafter. The person who is collecting *ajr*, if held accountable by Allah, will likely face loss, if he does not receive Allah's mercy. That's why the role of the *Wali* is not to teach how to accumulate rewards; rather, he teaches mercy and love. Rewards develop ruggedness in the person and keep him running after acts; "I should do this and not that, why did

I choose this over that?" Love is different; it teaches amiability and mercy. One will only see the mercy of Allah in everything and everyone. He will return every creature to Allah, the Creator, even if his mind rushes into thoughts. Unlike rewards, one links everything to acts.

Sidi Shaykh referred to a part of a saying of Moulay 'Abd al-Salam Ibn Mashish, in which he said: "Whoever guides you to awrad has tired you." Sidi Shaykh added that if one performs a particular dhikr 100 times, for example, he will receive as a reward a tree or an apartment in paradise. However, this approach is focused on acquiring material rewards, like building houses and apartments, which is tiring. Love, on the other hand, is different, it destroys everything. Even if one is offered paradise, he will not be interested. His worship is for the Lord of paradise, not for paradise itself. Similarly, regarding hell, he won't fear its fire, as his worship is for the Lord of the fire. This is Love, and this is why the Prophet ﷺ said: "They will have no fear when people will be struck with fear, and they will have no grief when people be struck with grief. Behold! The Awliya' of Allah, no fear shall come upon them, nor shall they grieve."[49]

If one is prostrating for an extended period just for the sake of getting a castle in paradise, perhaps because he is facing accommodation issues in his life. Similarly, if one prays for houris (*hur al-'ayn*), it may be due to problems with his wife. Thus, his prayers are a means to exchange places and people, there is no need to pretend love.

....

49   Al-Sijistani, Abu Dawud. *Sunan Abi Dawud.* #3527.

When one loves, his nights become days. He will walk towards Allah even without clothes, not considering any distractions. He remains in continuous remembrance of Allah, not seeking any reward, but because nothing in life interests him except the remembrance of Allah. The lover cares only about his beloved.

Sidi Shaykh finished this part by making a supplication (*du'a*): "O Allah grant us the heat of love, a heat that becomes coolness and safety as you did for Ibrahim, peace be upon him, so we dive into the sea of love until we see nothing but You, and thus realize the reality of 'Only Allah exists and nothing else.' O Allah protect us from the fire and darkness of our souls and its distractions."

Lecture 15.
December 23, 2022

*

The importance of having a Shaykh

Q: The importance of having a Shaykh.

Sidi Shaykh started this lecture by stating that realizing extinction or annihilation (*al-fana'*) in the Divine Presence doesn't come quickly, especially at the beginning of wayfaring (*suluk*). Every heart has its distractions, so one is always engaged in the greater jihad (*al-jihad al-akbar*), which is the *jihad* of the soul (*al-nafs*). That's why *ahl Allah* and Sufis stipulated that a Shaykh is essential in wayfaring to reveal to the disciple the diseases hidden in his heart, the way to heal from them, and to maintain a strong relationship with Allah.

The disciple takes this Shaykh as his Imam. In prayers, for example, the imam carries on those who pray behind him all of their mistakes and inattentions. It is similar for the Shaykh in the disciple's wayfaring (*suluk*). This is why

The Prophet ﷺ said: "Choose your imams as they are your intercessors on the Day of Resurrection."[50]

Hence, it is imperative to seek out a Shaykh who can lead one to the Divine Presence, saving him from the whims of his soul as well as the heedlessness and slips of his heart. To attain this state, the heart requires training and taming, as it represents a house and it can be a house for Allah as He has said: "Neither My Earth nor My Heavens could contain Me, whilst the heart of My believing servant does contain Me."[51]

Sidi Shaykh explained that Allah said My believing servant He did not refer to the muslim servant. Therefore, one needs to seek this station of Faith (*maqam al-iman*) which represents the middle of the three stations: The station of islam, the station of faith, and the station of excellence (*maqam al-ihsan*).

The station of islam is achieved with acts like prayer, fasting, etc. Then comes the station of faith which is based on the heart's deeds (*al-a'mal al-qalbiyyah*). The Prophet ﷺ described faith as having more than seventy branches and in another version of the Hadith, he ﷺ described it as having more than sixty branches. Both versions of the Hadith are correct, as the number of branches varies from one believing servant to another. When referring to branches, it is similar to academic branches. For instance, one chooses to

....

50   Al-Zurqani, Muhammad. *Sharh al-Zurqani 'Ala Muwatta' Imam Malik.* Vol. 1, "Your Imams are your intercessors"; Al-Bayhaqi, Abu Bakr. *Al-Sunan al-Kubra.* Vol. 1, Page 128, "Make your Imams from amongst your best".

51   Ibn 'Arabi, Muhyi al-Din. *Al-Futuhat al-Makiyyah.* Vol. 1, Page 216.

study the branch of physics another chooses the branch of mathematics. Faith is also a unique science with multiple branches.

From an apparent perspective, a believing servant believes in the six articles of faith but may not realize their reality. He requires a teacher to guide him through the different branches of faith. This path or this tunnel which is the niche of faith (*mishkat al-iman*) contains more than sixty or more than seventy stations to pass through, each one has its obstacles that decrease the level of faith and its good deeds that increase it. So, one needs a well-informed or an expert (*khabir*) to pass. As Allah said in the Quran: "**The All-Merciful. Ask about Him a well-informed.**"[52]

Sidi Shaykh added that it is not about words and talking, it is an experiential journey that one should pass through with the *Sunnah*. The Prophet ﷺ wasn't content with what he found from the earlier generations (*al-awalin*), so he returned to Allah, appealed to Him, and made the Cave of Hira his spiritual seclusion to contemplate and examine his inner and his relationship with himself and with his Lord.

When the command of Allah came to him ﷺ, it wasn't about words but rather science. Muslims are a nation (*umma*) of science (*'ilm*). The first word that came from Allah was "**read (*iqra'*)**". Hence, one is required to read these branches of faith, he should read them, but this reading is done with the heart, unlike the branches of islam that are recited with the tongue.

....

52   Quran 25:59.

The Prophet ﷺ provided the key to access the language and science of the heart. He said: "Hearts become rusty and are polished by the remembrance of Allah."[53] If studying every branch of faith requires specific remembrance (*dhikr*), then one will need more than sixty or seventy types of *dhikr* to purify the heart from the branches of the devil and restore it to the branches of faith.

Sidi Shaykh then said that if this *dhikr* reaches the heart, is it a *dhikr* with the tongue only? With tongue and vision? With all senses? One must know the way to enter the heart. If it is with tongue alone, it would be quite straightforward. One would simply engage in seventy types of remembrance, practice them diligently throughout the day, and that would suffice. Surely it doesn't work that way. The heart (*al-qalb*) of the body is its inner (*al-jawf*), not the organ itself. The heart, as an organ, serves as the gateway to access the inner body, the realm of faith; and the spiritual realm (*malakut*).

To reach one's inner self, distractions must be avoided. By distractions it is not just about falling into sins, these distractions should be avoided in the previous station, the station of islam. In the station of faith, one works on sincerity (*al-ikhlas*) and perfection of acts of worship (*'ibadah*) with a prerequisite that these acts are for the sake of Allah (*lillah*) not to brag about the number of prayers and *dhikr*. The folk of Allah (*ahl Allah*) were very careful about this. Some of them, before leaving their homes, would smear their beards with food to conceal their fasting. Others would

....

53   *Al-Khatib al-Tabrizi*, Muahammad Ibn 'Abdullah. *Mishkat al-Masabih*. #2168.

engage in the night prayer (*qiyam-al-layl*) all night long but sleep just before the Fajr prayer so that no one would know about their *qiyam*. These are deeds of the heart; they represent a gate between the servant and his Lord that no one shares with him.

The distracted (*al-multafit*) fails to understand the true essence of sincerity (*al-ikhlas*). This is why only the good deed (*al-'amal as-salah*) ascends to Allah. And when a good deed ascends to Allah, the righteous person (*al-'abd as-salah*) ascends with it. It is important to let go of good deeds once they're done. If someone keeps thinking about a good deed he did, like giving *sadaqah*, it indicates that the deed wasn't accepted.

This is what a distraction is, even in the midst of prayer at the mosque, one can still be a distracted person. Thus, one needs a *qibla* that keeps him directed to Allah. As long as one thinks that he is praying and doing *dhikr* that means that he has nothing. Allah is rich, He is not in need of the servant's deeds. Instead, good deeds originate from Allah and are attributed to His servants. One should consider this generosity, especially those who claim to be generous.

Sidi Shaykh referred to the Hadith of the Prophet ﷺ: "Verily, the hearts of all human beings are between two of the fingers of the All-Merciful as one heart; He turns it wherever He wills."[54] Hence, all of one's prayers with his faculties (*jawarah*) aim to ask Allah to keep his heart certain and steadfast on good deeds (*al-a'amal al-saliha*) and

....

54 *Sahih Muslim* #2655.

monotheism, rather than performing numerous deeds and prayers. The abundance of deeds, if undertaken without the branches of faith (*sh'uab al-iman*), may lead to vanity (*'ujub*).

The enemy of Muslims and of Allah, satan, used to pray as well. He prostrated to Allah across every inch of the earth which led to him being called azazil, ending with 'il' like other angels, such as Jibril and Mika'il. He was raised among angels and acquired knowledge with them until he was regarded as one of them. Allah called him the peacock of angels (*tawus al-mala'ika*). He prayed perfectly, but his heart was rusted. He received his share of the knowledge of the Divine Names (*'ilm al-asma'*) just like all angels did. The difference is that angels were sincere in their knowledge, but satan lost his sincerity. What he didn't lose were all the illnesses of the heart, which no one can count except Allah, who narrowed them down to three: envy (*hassad*), pride (*kibr*), and vanity (*'ujub*).

Sidi Shaykh explained that one should never deny the presence of these traits in him. This is what satan initially believed, until Adam, peace be upon him, was chosen as the vicegerent (*khalifa*) of Allah on earth, revealing the true nature of satan.

Lecture 16.
August 27, 2022

*

Seeking Allah through manifestations (*tajalliyat*)

Q: A disciple experienced a direct vision of Light (*musha-hada*), she described the Light as golden in color and shaped like a sun. Then she said: "It is a sun."

Sidi Shaykh responded that it is common in the Tariqa to perceive the Light as a sun, similar to the experience of Sayyiduna Ibrahim, peace be upon him. This is how Allah described the Light in the Quran: a star, a moon, and a sun.

Sidi Shaykh stated that saying "it is a sun" means that the disciple is in heedlessness and not present with Allah. Even if the disciple witnessed the manifestation (*al-tajalli*), he was not present with the Manifested (*al-mutajalli*). It was not the case for Sayyiduna Ibrahim, peace be upon him. He was present with Allah because when he saw the star, he said: "**This is my Lord.**" However, in this case, the disciple remained fixated on the image of the Light of Allah, which is His attribute, and forgot about the described which is Allah Himself.

111

The aim is not the vision of Light itself but to realize the reality of what one is seeing. If it were just a sun, everyone would see it as anyone can see the sun. However, Allah manifests Himself to people of piety (*ahl al-taqwa*) and people of the station of excellence (*maqam al-ihsan*).

This is why one should be aware of how he interprets what he sees. In the Tariqa, it is not considered sacred to see manifestations of the Light if one forgets about the Manifested (*al-mutajalli*). This is considered heedlessness. Allah didn't create the sun, the moon, or the heavens to remain fixated on them, but rather to know Him through these creations. As stated in the Quran: "**Those who remember Allah while standing, sitting, and lying on their sides, and reflect on the creation of the heavens and the earth.**"[55]

The ultimate objective is not reflecting on the creation of the heavens and the earth, but rather reaching the knowledge of Allah. When those who remember Allah and reflect on the creation of the heavens and the earth attained this knowledge they said: "**Our Lord! You have not created this without purpose. Glory be to You! Protect us from the torment of the fire.**"[56]

This is what is needed from disciples, but instead, they are bragging about their visions of Light and forgetting about their relationship with their Lord. It is not through this manner that one achieves something in the Tariqa; the true accomplishment is when one truly knows his Lord.

....

55   Quran 3:191.
56   Quran 3:191.

If one sees just the star and knows its origin, its language, its movement, how to interact with this star, and what this star is revealing to him from secrets, that's enough. He has realized the knowledge of Allah. On the other hand, seeing creations, staying with them, and forgetting about the Creator is just useless.

*

The six pointed and the octagonal stars

Q: A disciple saw in a dream an octagonal star with the Name "Allah" in its center.

Sidi Shaykh said that an octagonal star is a niche. Seeing the Name "Allah" in the center means that the knowledge of Allah comes when one enters the niche. It is clear from the verse of Light: "**Allah is the Light of the heavens and the earth. His Light is like a niche in which there is a lamp, the lamp is in a glass, the glass is like a shining star, lit from a Blessed Olive Tree.**"[57]

Regarding the geometric form, Sidi Shaykh stated that an octagonal star or a six-pointed star are both talismans of the universe. The six-pointed star is a talisman of the numbered Basmala (*al-basmala bil-marqum*). It is a triangle overlapped with another triangle that will give a six-pointed star and the shining star (*al-kawkab al-durri*) in the center. This

....

57   Quran 24:35.

talisman has seven points: six points of the star plus one in the center. The six-pointed star is called a hexa (*sudassi*), in reference to the six points of the star. In reality, it is a hepta (*suba'i*), as it has seven points. This is called the talisman of the universe, and it is built on time. Sidi Shaykh further explained that Allah created the heavens and the earth in six days, symbolized by the six points of the star. As for the center, it represents the Day of Increase (*yawm al-mazid*), known as Friday.

Sidi Shaykh added that this talisman is used for time calculation. While it is not necessary for the disciple to fully understand it, since the knowledge of Allah comes from the example of His Light, when someone begins to learn the science of time, he starts with this talisman as a beginner. Also, this talisman is constructed based on the Basmala, represented by three dots: the dot of the letter '*ba*', the dot of the letter 'nun', and the dot of the letter 'ya', which is two dots reassembled together. The three dots form a triangle which is the Basmala, the other triangle represents the shadow of the Basmala.

Sidi Shaykh stated regarding the disciple's dream that as long as it is a dream, it cannot be considered in this manner, as knowledge is received in the state of wakefulness and through perseverance in *dhikr*, *qiyam*, and fasting.

Sidi Shaykh continued the explanation of the talisman seen in the dream. He referred to the Hadith of the Prophet ﷺ: "Do not curse Time (*al-dahr*), for it is Allah Who is Time". This is why one can see the Name "Allah" in the talisman that represents time.

Sidi Shaykh then spoke about the octagonal star. He said that the octagonal star called *thumani* in Arabic, which translates to "an octa", is a square within a square. It is also built on the Basmala. The difference is that in the octagonal star, there is the dot of the letter 'ya' and its reflection. Thus, the letter 'ya' has two dots and the Basmala has four dots overall. This Basmala is called *al-basmala al-ka'bawiya*. It is used to measure place (*al-makan*).

When the dot appeared, it formed a square called *ka'bawiy*. Every *Basmala* needs its shadow. Someone might ask "Why does the *Basmala* require a shadow?" Simply put, it is because it is repeated 114 times in the Quran. If it didn't need a shadow, it would never be repeated 114 times.

The original Basmala is the Basmala of the Fatiha. There is no redundancy in the Quran; every Basmala in the Quran has its secret and significance. It indicates a time or a place. This particular Basmala indicates the place; this is why it is called *al-ka'bawiya*; it represents the *qibla* for everyone who is praying. It can be associated with the verse: **"Turn then Thy face in the direction of the sacred Mosque: Wherever ye are, turn your faces in that direction."**[58] As for the six-pointed star, or the hepta (*al-suba'i*), it can be associated with the verse: **"Whithersoever ye turn, there is the presence of Allah."**[59]

The octagonal star comprises eight points: four of them represent the letters of Ahmad in Arabic, while the other

....

58 Quran 2:144.
59 Quran 2:115.

four symbolize the four letters of Muhammad. Four by Four gives sixteen, so the origin of the octagonal star (*al-thumani*) is sixteen. This represents the measurement of place: seven heavens, seven earths, the throne, and the pedestal.

One might say that the heavens are not a place. Allah says in the Quran: **"And for a Garden whose width is that of the heavens and of the earth."**[60] Allah used both the heavens and the earth as a measurement for the width of the Garden, which means that the heavens and the earth are places.

Additionally, the Prophet ﷺ said: "The first heaven compared to the second heaven, is like a small ring thrown into a desert. The second heaven compared to the third heaven, is like a small ring thrown into a desert [...] The seventh heaven compared to the Footstool (*kursi*) ring is like a small ring thrown into a desert, and the Footstool compared to the Throne (*'arsh*) is like a small ring thrown into a desert."[61] Using the term desert to describe the heavens indicates that the Prophet ﷺ is indeed referring to the heavens as places.

When the disciple gathers the rings of the heavens, he is in fact gathering place, not time. But when he starts to work on diffraction (*fatq*) and the condensed state (*ratq*), he is working on time. The Shaykh teaches the disciple diffraction (*fatq*) and the undifferentiated stitching (*ratq*), which means that he teaches him how to fold time and place. If a Shaykh does not master this science, he is not considered a Shaykh. It is a science, not a myth or just thoughts. It is

....

60 Quran 57:21.
61 Al-Alussi, Muhammad. *Ruh al-Ma'ani Fi Tafsir al-Sab'u al-Mathani.*

a science much like the science of 1+1=2. In this science, the octagonal star is for beginners similar to learning the alphabet.

The center of the octagonal star is identical to that of the six-pointed star. This similarity often confuses others, as both the science of time and the science of place have the same center.

Sidi Shaykh referred to the Hadith of Sayyiduna Ali, may Allah honor his face: "All what is in the Quran is included in the Fatiha, and all what is in the Fatiha is included in *Bism Allah al-Rahman al-Rahim*, and all what is in *Bism Allah al-Rahman al-Rahim* is included in *Bism Allah*, and all what is in *Bism Allah* is included in the '*Ba*', and the secret of the *Ba* is the dot, and I am the Dot."

Sidi Shaykh added that the Quran contains stories (*qasas*). These stories inform about time and place. So, projecting the Hadith of Sayyiduna Ali, may Allah honor his face, it can be said that the whole time and place are in the *Basmala*, and the whole time and place are in *Bism Allah*, and the whole time and place are in the '*Ba*' and the secret of time and place are in the Dot and I am the secret of time and place. That's what Sayyiduna Ali, may Allah honor his face, wanted to inform. He is the center of time and place, the center of the six-pointed and octagonal stars.

Sidi Shaykh reaffirmed at the end of his response that this is considered in the case of visions, not dreams.

Lecture 17.
January 14, 2023

*

Witnessing the full moon

Q: A disciple stated that he suddenly woke up from sleeping, and when he closed his eyes, he saw the Light in the form of a full moon.

Sidi Shaykh started his response by mentioning that new disciples should watch previous lectures to help themselves understand their wayfaring (*suluk*). He added that disciples have two types of remembrance: The litany (*al-wird*) and the unlimited remembrance (*dhikr mutlaq*). The response of Allah, which is the manifestation of the Divine Light, can occur either during remembrance or afterward. When the disciple is not practicing remembrance, as in the case of sleeping, and he receives the manifestation (*al-tajalli*), he should begin engaging in *dhikr*. That is how one can understand what he is seeing. On the other hand, if one simply remains fixated on the vision, he will gain nothing from it. The remembrance that he practices serves as a form of magnification (*ta'dhim*) for the manifestation.

Regarding the vision, Sidi Shaykh stated that the Light has the form of a star, a moon, and a sun, similar to the experience of Sayyiduna Ibrahim, peace be upon him. When he saw the moon and it set, he said: **"I do not love things that set"**[62]. One should be just like Sayyiduna Ibrahim, not in sayings, but if the moon sets, one must feel empty and sad. If one feels bad for the absence of the moon, it will return bigger, like a sun, next time. However, the vision may never return if its absence doesn't affect one. The aim is not the vision itself but to know the Manifested (*al-mutajalli*) through the manifestation (*al-tajalli*).

*

There is no knowledge without the *Wali*

Q: A disciple had a dream vision (*ru'ya*) where he was sitting next to Sidi Shaykh. Sidi Shaykh mentioned that he would reveal the first six secrets to him, along with two other disciples sitting in front of him. As Sidi Shaykh began the *dhikr* of the Name "Allah", he turned his attention to the other two disciples, leaving the third disciple behind. Suddenly, a wall of gold was built between the disciple at the back and Sidi Shaykh, yet the disciple could still see them through

....

62 Quran 6:76.

the wall. Eventually, the wall disappeared, and Sidi Shaykh returned to the disciple at the back, continuing to invoke the Name "Allah".

Sidi Shaykh stated that the message here is clear: the secrets are within the Name "Allah" and within the Shaykh. Invoking the Name "Allah" without the Shaykh is not sufficient. Without the Shaykh, there will be no lecture of the Name, nor science, nor secrets, nor Sainthood (*wilaya*). Even if one invokes the Name "Allah", his share, he receives it from the Shaykh, as stated by the Prophet ﷺ in a Hadith: "Allah is the Giver and I am the distributor (*al-Qasim*)."[63]

The knowledge arises when both the *Wali* and the Name are present. That's why Allah says in the Quran: "**Allah is the *Wali* of those who believe. He brings them out from darkness into Light.**"[64] He did not say "Allah brings those who believe from darkness into Light" but rather He added the word "*Wali*".

When the disciple hears about the example of the Divine Light, he feels a strong desire to see it. Yet, he forgot that the *Wali* is the Example of the Divine Light: The niche, the lamp, the glass, and the shining star. If one does not consider the *Wali*, he does not have a relationship with him, and does not follow him, he will never see the example of the Divine Light. Simply because denying the *Wali* in the physical realm (*mulk*), results in being denied by the *Wali* in

....

63　*Sahih Bukhari* #3116.
64　Quran 2:257.

the spiritual realm (*malakut*). Vice versa, If one recognizes the *Wali* in the physical realm, the *Wali* recognizes him in the spiritual realm.

The Prophet ﷺ said: "My intercession is for the people who committed major sins in My Nation (*ummah*)"[65]. These people have committed major sins and mistakes in their lives, but they recognize the Messengerhood (*risala*) of the Messenger of Allah. This is why they are eligible for his intercession.

Sidi Shaykh said about the Shaykh giving his back to the disciple while facing the two other disciples in the dream vision that the Light has no direction. The Light comes wherever, whenever, and to whoever the Light wants. No place or time can limit the Light. It is the same for the *Wali*, the manifestations (*al-tajalliyyat*), including the example of the Divine Light, come from the presence of the *Wali* in the spiritual realm (*malakut*). Thus, the *Wali* should be regarded as superior to manifestations. The *Wali*, that the disciple connects and communicates with through the Light, has no direction. That's why Allah says: **"lit from a Blessed Olive Tree, neither to the east nor the west"**[66]. Directions are for the disciple, for the one at the receiving end, as for the Light, it has no direction. The gate of the niche is the heavens and the earth. If one removes them, he will find no direction within the niche. By removing them,

....

65 *Jami' al-Tirmidhi* #2435.
66 Quran 24:35.

he only removes himself. However, if one removes the *Wali*, as some do, he eliminates the Example of Light. Then, he finds only darkness.

In every action one pursues, he should recognize the *Wali*'s role, as the *Wali* brought him from the darkness of his soul (*nafs*) to the Light. Maybe beforehand he was praying, but he was just fulfilling a duty, not really praying because the Prophet ﷺ said: "Prayer is Light."[67] Hence, one needs the *Wali* to bring him to the Light of prayer. The disciple needs the *Wali* in worship acts, in faith, and in the station of excellence. The reason that one is not receiving this spiritual flow (*madad*) is that he does not recognize the *Wali* and does not acknowledge the benefactor. As a result, he lost the Light of prayer, of fasting, and of knowledge and he slowly fell into darkness.

If one loves the *Wali* more than oneself, never denies him even in his thoughts, and takes him as a *qibla*, then he will receive the spiritual flow. But if one's relationship with the *Wali* is for something, then one will stay in the station of reward (*ajr*). Even if the *Wali* gives him something, he should know that the *Wali* doesn't want him and doesn't even consider him.

The heavens and the earth, if placed on one side, and the example of the Light of Allah on the other, who must submit to the other? Surely, it is the heavens and the earth that should submit. The Light of the heavens and the earth doesn't even acknowledge them. It is the same for the human

....

67   *Sahih Muslim* #223.

being, consisting of a body and a spirit. The body must submit to the soul because the soul is considered the command of Lordship. Otherwise, the body will fall into darkness and be considered nonexistent. Allah says in the Quran: **"Is he who was dead and We have raised him unto life, and set for him a light wherein he walketh among men"**[68]. So, without the Light, the body is just dead.

....

68   Quran 6:122.

Lecture 18.
January 18, 2023

*

Sidi Shaykh's spiritual seclusion (*kholwa*)

Q: A disciple asked Sidi Shaykh about his experience in spiritual seclusion (*kholwa*).

Sidi Shaykh replied that while he had already shared how he started his path and how his Shaykh had accepted to admit him into the spiritual seclusion, not everything that occurred there could be revealed.

Sidi Shaykh said that since his childhood, his father, Moulay al-Tayeb, may Allah be pleased with him, would regularly visit their relatives on every Muslim holy day, taking them along each time. On one occasion, it was Eid al-Fitr when they visited Haj al-Hassan, may Allah's mercy be upon him, the uncle of Sidi Shaykh, may Allah sanctify his secret, who would later become his Shaykh.

As usual, a conversation ensued. al-Haj al-Hassan used to discuss various subjects on these kinds of occasions; sometimes He talked about agriculture, industry, etc. This time, the conversation revolved around Saints (*awliya'*) and the Names and Attributes of Allah.

The conversation primarily involved al-Haj al-Hassan, two of his children who were graduates in Islamic jurisprudence and academic studies, and a brother of al-Haj al-Hassan who also had an academic background.

A debate started as the discourse of al-Haj al-Hassan, may Allah's mercy be upon him, was not to their liking. They presented arguments such as how a Muslim can know his Lord through the five pillars of Islam, etc. On the other hand, al-Haj al-Hassan was talking about *dhikr* of the Name of Majesty Allah, and how one can reach the love and knowledge of Allah through this *dhikr*.

In his talk, al-Haj al-Hassan was not attempting to prove them wrong, but rather to suggest to them that in addition to what they already knew, there might be another door open for the love of Allah, one that doesn't necessarily rely on previous knowledge or information.

Sidi Shaykh was amazed by the talk of al-Haj al-Hassan, as if he were savoring every word. Despite the others presenting arguments and scientific references, he didn't even hear them. Their talking was a nuisance to him, and he perceived vanity and wonder in them.

The way al-Haj al-Hassan made the relationship with Allah very simple, amazed Sidi Shaykh. He referenced stories of people like Rabi'a al-'Adawiya and al-Fudayl to illustrate how the relationship with Allah can be simple, emphasizing that sincerity and honesty are sufficient to get Allah's response, without relying on previous knowledge or information.

Sidi Shaykh stated that he didn't need proof or a reference to trust al-Haj al-Hassan, who demonstrated step by step, in a very simple way, how Allah can accept repentance. Not only that, but He, al-Haj al-Hassan, also added that this acceptance is confirmed with evidence that one receives from Allah. This evidence manifests in the form of visions. Sidi al-Haj al-Hassan also explained these visions. He said that one can see the Name of Majesty "Allah" manifested in Light, and that's sufficient for repentance and for knowledge of Allah.

When the conversation came to an end, Sidi al-Haj al-Hassan left the room, and Sidi Shaykh followed him, asking if Allah would accept his repentance. al-Haj al-Hassan responded that Allah accepts everyone's repentance except if one associates partners with Him.

Then he said to Sidi Shaykh that Allah already accepted his repentance and started to cry. He knew that Sidi Shaykh, may Allah sanctify his secret, didn't pronounce these words randomly, certainly there was a secret behind them.

In the earlier conversation, al-Haj al-Hassan spoke about the remembrance (*dhikr*) of the Name "Allah" and that one needs to obtain permission to invoke the Name. He also spoke about the spiritual seclusion (*al-kholwa*). Sidi Shaykh then requested permission from him to engage in *dhikr* of the Name "Allah" and to be admitted into the spiritual seclusion.

Al-Haj al-Hassan agreed and said to Sidi Shaykh that when he comes to al-Aroui, where Sidi Shaykh lived at that time, he will give him *al-wasita* to invoke the Name

"Allah" and after a period he will admit him into the spiritual seclusion.

[Note: *al-wasita* is a table in which the Name "Allah" is written. The disciple put in front of him when engaging in remembrance of the Name "Allah". It was used in the Tariqa of al-Haj al-Hassan and with the first disciples of Sidi Shaykh, may Allah sanctify his secret.]

From al-Haj al-Hassan's words, Sidi Shaykh assumed that he had permission to invoke the Name "Allah". He returned to the room while al-Haj al-Hassan left to pray the Isha prayer. Sidi Shaykh began invoking the Name "Allah", while others started singing poems. Then, the sacred dance (*al-hadra*) started. It was the first time Sidi Shaykh, may Allah sanctify his secret, initiated the *hadra* himself.

After the Hadra, Moulay al-Tayeb and Sidi Shaykh took their vehicle to return home. It was around 11 pm; Moulay al-Tayeb was driving, with the cousin of Sidi Shaykh in the front seat, while Sidi Shaykh was in the back. During this road trip, Sidi Shaykh received the first sign.

While Sidi Shaykh engaged in his *dhikr*, the others were talking about jinns and the Zawiya of Sidi Shaykh's grandfather, Moulay al-Taher al-Karkari, reminiscing about how it had become desolate. The cousin was convincing Moulay al-Tayeb of the existence of a ghost in the Zawiya, despite Moulay al-Tayeb's denial of this story.

Suddenly, Sidi Shaykh saw a donkey tied up in the wild. Sidi Shaykh knew that in these kinds of places, animals should be taken to the stable by the time of the Maghrib prayer. So, he feared for the child who left the donkey there, assuming that he would be punished by his parents. After about three minutes, Sidi Shaykh saw the same donkey tied up, but from the other side of the road. He immediately realized that the donkey was from the world of jinn. Sidi Shaykh rejoiced not because he saw revelations from the other world, but because there wasn't a child who would be punished.

He understood the message of Allah, that with the remembrance of Allah, one can receive a response to anything, especially to the conversation that was happening in the car. He understood that jinns exist and can be seen. He didn't think that the donkey was a jinn, but rather that it was the property of a jinn.

After arriving home, Sidi Shaykh kept invoking the Name of Allah until the Subh prayer. In the morning, he went to work with his father, Moulay al-Tayeb. After the Duhr prayer, while he was sitting under an orange tree in the garden of his father's clinic, he felt tightness and discomfort. He felt that all he wanted was to visit al-Haj al-Hassan and enter the spiritual seclusion.

Knowing his father, Sidi Shaykh assumed that it would be hard to convince him to let him travel to Temsamane, where al-Haj al-Hassan lives. He would certainly refuse. Surprisingly, Moulay Tayeb agreed to let him go, and when Sidi Shaykh said that the reason was his desire to enter the *kholwa*, Moulay Tayeb started to cry.

After obtaining his father's agreement to travel to Temsamane, Sidi Shaykh returned home to find his mother preparing the table for lunch. She asked him where his father was. Sidi Shaykh replied that his father would arrive soon. She then invited him to wait for her to have lunch together, but he refused and informed her that he was going to travel to Temsamane. She proposed to him to give him his lunch, but he said that he had no time. Sidi Shaykh went down to his room to prepare for his trip.

He opened his closet to find clothes, but all he had were fashion items like jeans and sportswear. He started wondering how he could enter the *kholwa* with such clothes. If he couldn't even go to the mosque dressed like this, how could he enter the *kholwa*, which he considered even more sacred, with such clothes?

He decided to burn everything that couldn't be used to go to the mosque. He reasoned that if he couldn't go to the mosque with those items, how could he give them to someone else? Then he put up what remained for donation.

He found himself with only two items: a cloak belonging to his brother, Sidi Ahmad, and a jilbab belonging to his father, Moulay al-Tayeb. He was surprised because all he had left was not his own. It was as if he had shed a part of his past. Sidi Shaykh then wore some old sandals and packed all his diplomas and souvenirs in a small suitcase.

At this point, he had nothing left except his phone. He removed the SIM card, broke it, and gave the phone to his mother before leaving the house. Wanting to confirm his own commitment, he went to the barber to shave off all of his beard and hair. Sidi Shaykh decided to remove his beard because the beard gives the appearance of a faithful person.

Sidi Shaykh's first stop on his trip was a small village called Ben Tayeb. Upon his arrival, it was time for the Asr prayer, so he went to the mosque where he always prayed when traveling to Temsamane.

When he entered the mosque, it was still empty. There was a big board in the *mihrab* with the Name "Allah" written on it. He prayed some supererogatory prayers in front of the Name, then he joined the congregation for the Asr prayer led by the imam before leaving.

After leaving the mosque, Sidi Shaykh paid attention to his suitcase and felt that it represented a great burden for him, as he wanted to sever ties with the past. He then bought a lighter and set everything in the suitcase on fire, keeping only the one in which he placed his brother's cloak. Although he was supposed to take another taxi to reach Temsamane, he decided to continue his journey on foot. He also made the decision to remove his sandals and continue the path barefoot. He realized that the more he suffers to achieve his goal, the better the result will be.

At that time, Sidi Shaykh was putting on the hood of the cloak that was hiding him. He decided to take it off so that everyone would recognize him. He kept walking, sometimes looking up at the sky, sometimes down at the ground. Suddenly, after a while, Allah sent him a Light brighter than the sun. The sky became filled with this intense Light that he could no longer see the ground.

At that moment, Sidi Shaykh didn't realize that it was Light; he believed that Allah had accepted his repentance but had taken his sight as a consequence. Anticipating complete blindness, he hurried to reach his uncle's house as quickly as possible.

At that time, he didn't fear much because his ten years of wandering (*siyaha*) had taught him to adapt to any situation, like walking for long distances and sleeping anywhere. The only fear that remained in him was of dogs, as he had been bitten by one when he was a child. Coincidentally, a dog crossed his path and began to attack him. It wasn't a skinny street dog, but a large, well-bred one. Sidi Shaykh thought to himself that if being eaten by the dog meant his repentance would be fully accepted, he was okay with it. The dog started to move back and forth and attacked him exactly where he had been bitten in the past. At that moment, the last trace of fear vanished completely.

Suddenly, the dog's demeanor changed, and it began to show affection towards Sidi Shaykh, accompanying him on his walk as though he were its owner. It walked with Sidi Shaykh for a while until the dog's family appeared and reclaimed it.

After a moment, Sidi Shaykh arrived, and al-Haj al-Hassan opened the door for him. He already knew that Sidi Shaykh was coming because a member of his family had seen him in the village. He was with his son, named Taher, and Sidi Ibn al-Sini, a disciple of al-Haj al-Hassan who later became a disciple of Sidi Shaykh. Sidi Shaykh ran towards al-Haj al-Hassan and tried to kiss his foot, but al-Haj al-Hassan pushed him away aggressively. Then he instructed his son to accompany Sidi Shaykh to the bus station and see him off. However, Sidi Shaykh refused and informed al-Haj al-Hassan that he had no intention of returning home. He explained that after wandering the earth for ten years, he now intends to continue his journey at sea if he isn't accepted. This is when al-Haj al-Hassan accepted him and instructed him to wash himself from the dust. He told him to consider what to do with him later.

Sidi Shaykh spent the rest of the day with the family. He prayed and dined with them. When it was time to sleep, al-Haj al-Hassan called Sidi Shaykh, gave him a rosary (*subha*), and they made the pledge of allegiance (*al-bay'ah*).

Sidi Shaykh didn't understand the purpose of the pledge of allegiance at that time, nor did he know about the litany (*al-wird*) or its significance. When he woke up during the last third of the night, he began to see the Light again on the prayer carpet, but he still didn't recognize it as the Divine Light.

Afterward, he picked up the Quran, opened it, and attempted to read Surah al-Tawba, but he encountered many difficulties as he couldn't see the letters clearly due to the overwhelming brightness of the Light. He then prayed the Subh prayer and engaged in the remembrance of seeking forgiveness (*istighfar*) since he didn't know the litany.

In the morning, Sidi Shaykh heard his Shaykh instructing his daughter to prepare a room, indicating his intention to use it as a guest chamber in the future. It was then that Sidi Shaykh realized he would be entering into the spiritual seclusion.

After the discussion that took place between al-Haj al-Hassan and his daughter, he called Sidi Shaykh, may Allah sanctify his secret, asking him if he wanted them to prepare breakfast for him. Sidi Shaykh replied that he was fasting, so he was immediately admitted into spiritual seclusion.

Sidi Shaykh described the place as a small room, with the *dhikr* spot positioned in a way that made reclining in any direction uncomfortable. Sidi Shaykh said that it resembles a grave. The first instruction al-Haj al-Hassan gave to Sidi Shaykh, may Allah sanctify his secret, was that sleeping is forbidden. After al-Haj al-Hassan left, Sidi Shaykh started his remembrance.

Instead of invoking the Name "Allah", Sidi Shaykh engaged in *istighfar*. For him, the primary reason for his seclusion was to seek forgiveness from Allah. All he wanted at that time was to hear the words "I forgave you (*laqad ghafartu lak*)."

From the time of Dhuha until the Asr prayer, al-Haj al-Hassan was instructing Sidi Shaykh to invoke the Name "Allah". However, as soon as al-Haj al-Hassan leaves, Sidi Shaykh returns to engaging in *istighfar*. Then al-Haj al-Hassan explained to Sidi Shaykh that the Name of Majesty "Allah", includes every form of remembrance, such as saying *astaghfiru Allah, Bismillah al-Rahman al-Rahim*, and so on. It was at this point that Sidi Shaykh began to invoke the Name "Allah".

Later in the day, al-Haj al-Hassan entered the *kholwa* and asked Sidi Shaykh if he saw something. Sidi Shaykh started to describe what he was seeing at that very moment while talking to his Shaykh. The space in the *kholwa* resembled a three-dimensional piece of art, with the Name "Allah" written in various fonts and colors.

After giving him some instructions, al-Haj al-Hassan left and didn't turn off the light. Sidi Shaykh continued his *dhikr* with the light on; he didn't dare to turn it off as his Shaykh left it that way. Sidi Shaykh was still seeing the Name even with the light on, which he told his Shaykh when he came back to check on him. He then gave him new instructions about ascending and also provided him with some food to break his fast. Afterward, he turned off the light and left.

Sidi Shaykh continued his *dhikr* with great diligence. He then experienced the first manifestation (*tajalli*): he saw himself in al-Aroui, in a place with raw ground, rocks, etc. However, Allah revealed to him the grave of a *Wali* in that place. At that moment, al-Haj al-Hassan came to check on Sidi Shaykh, may Allah sanctify his secret, but he didn't find him there. He searched for him in every corner, even in the bathroom, but could not find him. When he returned later and asked him where he was, Sidi Shaykh told him that he was there and informed him about what he experienced.

When Sidi Shaykh understood what happened, he realized that he could move to other places while engaging in *dhikr*. This motivated him greatly to stay awake that night. From that point on, he experienced numerous manifestations that he could not disclose, as he mentioned, but he described them as beautiful (*jamal*).

After Sidi Shaykh recounted his experiences to al-Haj al-Hassan, the latter instructed him to leave the *kholwa*.

Despite al-Haj al-Hassan's request, Sidi Shaykh didn't want to leave, leading his Shaykh to allow him to stay for one more night.

Before Sidi Shaykh left the *kholwa*, al-Haj al-Hassan sat down in front of him. He drew the Name "Allah" with the dot on top of the *'alif* and explained to Sidi Shaykh that the dot represents the treasure. He further elaborated that the dot had flowed and written the *'alif*, the two 'lams', and the 'ha'. Sidi Shaykh understood then everything he passed through and left the *kholwa* crying.

After his *kholwa*, Sidi Shaykh spent several months visiting graves, crying, and praying to Allah. Then Allah revealed to him the proof that he was eligible for his path. After that, he spent a long period reading the book of Shaykh Ibn 'Ajiba, "Awakening Aspirations - Commentary on al-Hikam of Shaykh Ibn 'Ata Allah." Sidi Shaykh explained that he reflected on every aphorism (*hikma*), allowing him to contemplate and meditate with *dhikr* on various concepts such as the sun, the human body, and more.

He realized that through *dhikr*, he could comprehend any concept. He also realized that true knowledge remains accessible as long as one does not alter or distort it, nor claim something contrary to its essence.

Sidi Shaykh also focused on the saying of Sayyiduna Ali, may Allah honor his face, where he said: "I am the Dot." He began reflecting on every dot in the Quran, trying to perceive Sayyiduna Ali, may Allah honor his face, in them. After a while, he received a revelation from a dot in surah al-Waqi'a, written in the Kufi style. Another aspect shared by Sidi Shaykh is that he reached a stage where he created clones of himself to engage in gatherings of *dhikr* with them.

He enjoyed being alone. His days started at midnight when he woke up for *qiyam*, and he spent most of his day in *dhikr* until *al-Isha* prayer. Revelations and manifestations became common for him. When he read the Quran, he found everything he experienced reflected in its verses. That's when he fell in love with the Quran, a love that continues until today.

To conclude, Sidi Shaykh stated that during his seclusion, he obtained knowledge of Allah, and after his seclusion, he acquired knowledge of the Prophet ﷺ and recognized how the Prophet is a mercy for all creation. He added that everything one seeks to see in visions and revelations is included in the Quran.

Lecture 19.
January 28, 2023

*

Vision of the Shaykh during the litany (*al-wird*)

Q: During her *wird* practice, a disciple had a direct vision in which she saw Sidi Shaykh, may Allah sanctify his secret, wearing a green cloak (*jilbab*), a red hat, and antimony to blacken the edges of his eyes as an adornment (*kohl*).

Sidi Shaykh said that a vision of a *Wali* is a reality. The Prophet ﷺ said: "Whoever sees me in a dream will see me in his wakefulness, and satan cannot imitate Me in shape."[69] Thus, when someone sees the *Wali* in a dream means that he has seen the Prophet ﷺ in the presence of Sainthood (*wilaya*), or one could say, from the perspective of Sainthood.

One should not imagine that when The Prophet ﷺ said: "Whoever sees me in a dream will see me in his wakefulness", it implies seeing him physically walking in the physical realm (*mulk*). While this is possible, the intended meaning is that

....

69   *Sahih Bukhari* #6993.

139

one will see him in the closest image to him, which is that of *Ahl al-Bayt*. In this case, it is the image of the Shaykh.

Sidi Shaykh added that seeing the Shaykh depends on the disciple's state. If he sees him when he is in the physical realm (*mulk*), it means that he is seeing the key to the entrance to the spiritual realm (*malakut*). If he sees him in the spiritual realm, it means that he is seeing the key to the entrance to the realm of invincibility (*jabarut*). And if he sees him in the realm of invincibility, it means that he is seeing the secret of the Essence. In reality, the disciple requires the Shaykh wherever he may be: in the physical realm (*mulk*), the spiritual realm (*malakut*), or the realm of invincibility (*jabarut*).

Sidi Shaykh further elaborated on the significance of the green jilbab, explaining that the green color symbolizes the manifestation of the reunion of the Divine Names (*jam'iyat al-asma'*). He likened it to viewing the glass (*al-zujaja*) from a distance, allowing one to see all of its sides simultaneously. It means that if all the Names are united together, they will reflect the green color in the glass. As for the red hat, Sidi Shaykh explained that the red color represents the Divine Name the Death-Causer (*al-Mumit*), and the hat symbolizes a crown on the head of the *Wali*. Thus, the glass is reflecting the red color and the *Wali* is wearing a crown.

Regarding the kohl, Sidi Shaykh mentioned that the *Wali* had it in his eyes. Surely, it is a *Sunnah* of the Prophet ﷺ and is also used as a remedy for the eyes. However, in this instance, the disciple focused on the outward appearance of the *Wali's* eyes.

The Prophet ﷺ said in a Hadith: "Be aware of the believer's intuition for indeed he sees with Allah's light."[70] It can be said that a believer has seventy degrees of vision, whereas a normal person has only one. Thus, this believer's eye or sight can pierce through seventy veils, each corresponding to one of the seventy branches of faith.

Every branch is a veil that the believer servant can pierce until he reaches the last veil, which is the last branch of faith: *la ilaha illa Allah*. This doesn't imply that *la ilah illa Allah* is a veil itself, but rather, the vision of the believer servant to *la ilaha illa Allah* is considered as a veil.

Sidi Shaykh explained that the disciple here remained with the first degree of the eye of the Shaykh and didn't pierce any of his veils. He also noted that some disciples have been able to go beyond some of these veils. For instance, when they see the hand or the foot of the Shaykh, they may see more than the outward appearance.

....

70 *Jami' al-Tirmidhi* #3127.

*

How to deal with intrusive thoughts

Q: A disciple inquired about dealing with intrusive thoughts during acts of worship. For instance, when he intends his actions for the sake of Allah (*lillah*), but then doubts arise, suggesting that he may be performing them for self-glorification. He sought advice on overcoming these thoughts and whether they impact the acceptance of his deeds by Allah.

Sidi Shaykh explained that the thoughts that occur during acts of worship are whispers (*waswasa*) from satan. While the acts of worship are still accepted and the disciple will get the reward (*ajr*) for them, what is affected is the disciple's presence and connection with Allah. The more one has thoughts, the more he is distant from Allah, and vice versa.

Sidi Shaykh provided a concrete example, explaining that in the case of prayer, satan can use thoughts and whispers, suggesting that the disciple is only perfecting his prayer to impress others. As a first reaction, one may rush through the prayer to counter those thoughts. However, the correct approach is to prolong the prayer by taking more time in bowing (*ruku'*) and prostration (*sujud*). This way, the door is shut to satan and his whispers.

Sidi Shaykh added that if thoughts occur when reading the Quran during prayers, the best reaction is to recite the Quran aloud, focusing on listening to its recitation rather than hearing whispers. He also recommended reading the Quran aloud in the prayers of *qiyam*. Also, it is beneficial for the disciple during bowing and prostration, to cry and complain to Allah about his weaknesses, seeking His help. Allah will grant the strength needed to overcome satan and his whispers.

Sidi Shaykh added that when whispers (*waswasa*) occur, it affects sincerity in the prayer. However, the disciple can still focus on perfecting his prayers because doing so will ultimately lead to sincerity.

*

The importance of preaching (*da'wa*)

Q: A disciple had a dream vision of traveling and teaching about the Tariqa in Mauritania. Then he remembered his father. When he came back to check on him, he found Sidi Shaykh holding his hand.

Sidi Shaykh said that disciples who live abroad, are distant from their families, and are working, should not forget the right of *Ahl al-Bayt* upon them, which is to preach to Allah and His Messenger. The disciple should set aside a specific time, for example, once a week, to work on this.

Sidi Shaykh added that it is not by chance that the dream occurred in Mauritania, perhaps this region specifically requires this particular disciple's attention and efforts. This doesn't necessarily imply that he needs to travel there, the internet can be useful for sharing the Shaykh's teachings, videos of disciples, and all information about the Tariqa.

*

The vision of the star, the moon, and the sun

Q: A disciple asked about how the Light can be in the form of a sun.

Sidi Shaykh explained that when it comes to direct vision (*mushahada*), the disciple should take no account of what he feels or his interpretations. When the Light appears in the form of the sun, it is bright and clear, like the sun during Duhr prayer time in the physical realm (*mulk*). The same applies to the moon and the star, they are as clear as they appear in the sky in the physical realm.

Sidi Shaykh added that when the disciple engages in *dhikr* in the last third of the night and sees the moon resembling a full moon, he can consider himself among the monotheists (*al-muwahidin*). This is better than writing and reading books, etc. Additionally, if he sees a sun just like he sees the sun during Duhr's time, then he can consider himself as the sun of knowledge.

Sidi Shaykh explained that the vision of Light isn't about feelings but about what the disciple sees. It is similar to the experience of Sayyiduna Ibrahim, peace be upon him. When he saw the star, he said: "**This is my Lord.**" When he saw the moon, he said: "**This is my Lord.**" And when he saw the sun, he said: "**This is my Lord.**" Allah didn't blame him for what he said; on the contrary, Allah reported it in the Quran as an example for Muslims to follow.

*

Reciting the Quranic *wird*

Q: A disciple asked whether he can read the Surahs of the Quranic *wird* which are Yassin, al-Fath, al-Rahman, al-Waqi'a, al-Hadid, and al-Mulk, altogether, or if it would be better to split them, reciting four in the morning and two in the evening.

Sidi Shaykh stated that the program in the Zawiya is built to be balanced between morning and evening. This is because the disciples in the Zawiya have time, but if the disciple has work, family, etc., he can read them altogether. The aim is to read them at least once a day.

Sidi Shaykh added that each of these Surahs is chosen for a reason. For example, the Prophet ﷺ said that whoever perseveres on Surah al-Mulk gets his intercession on the Day of Resurrection. Also, Surah al-Waqi'a is for sustenance (*rizq*), etc.

Lecture 20.
February 4, 2023

*

Talking to the image of the Shaykh

Q: A disciple stated that after experiencing injustice, she cried and talked to a picture of Sidi Shaykh to tell him what happened. That night, she dreamt of a man giving her a drink of water. When she woke up, she felt calm and happy. The following day, the same man reached out to her on social media, leaving her pleasantly surprised and happy about what happened.

Sidi Shaykh said that a dream (*ru'ya*) is from Allah. What happens in a dream might happen in the physical realm (*mulk*) and is just a premonition of what is to come, whether it is good or bad. He added that if the heart was calmed down by this dream, it means that it is a good thing. Depending on the faith of the person, Allah gives him a dream to calm his heart.

Sidi Shaykh added that speaking with the image of the Shaykh is neither mandatory nor prohibited; it depends on the spiritual state of the disciple. Some may see it as a strange thing to do, but in reality, it depends on the disciple's relationship and belief in the spiritual reality of the Shaykh, and if he has exalted the Shaykh's spiritual reality in his heart. However, If the disciple did not reach this spiritual state, he is not obligated to do it.

Sidi Shaykh said that even the Shaykh may experience this. For example, when visiting the tombs of some Saints, he may even kiss the walls of the tomb, cry, and talk to them. He added that this is the best language, the language of the spirit and of the heart, which occurs between the disciple and whom he trusts and considers as the key to salvation. Some disciples always feel the presence of the Shaykh in *dhikr*, in prayers, etc. They are constantly in connection with their Shaykh. It does not imply that they worship or prostrate to the Shaykh. Rather, submitting to the Shaykh is a matter of education and demonstrating respect towards him. This is a well-known aspect of the Tariqa and not something to be kept secret.

However, worship is only reserved for Allah. The respect and obedience demonstrated towards the Shaykh in behavior are similar to the respect and obedience shown to one's parents. On a deeper level, it resembles the obedience of the body to the spirit, as the body cannot function without the spirit.

Sidi Shaykh commented on the disciple's dream and explained that even if the dream is realized in the physical realm (*mulk*), it doesn't mean that a woman has permission to privately talk to men. It is mandatory to respect the

Islamic law when dealing with and communicating with the opposite gender, especially for older women who may refer to men as their son or their brothers. This may not necessarily be reciprocated from the other side.

*

Facing social challenges in the spiritual journey

Q: A disciple mentioned that he was experiencing difficulties in his relationships with people. Recently, he began to pray, imploring Allah through the Prophet ﷺ and Sidi Shaykh, may Allah sanctify his secret, to assist him in his interactions with others and to protect him from hypocritical and wicked people. He noticed a significant improvement in his situation, and his relationships with others became much better.

Sidi Shaykh emphasized that supplication (*du'a*) is highly beneficial as it draws the servant closer to his Lord, and Allah indeed loves to be invoked by His servants. Furthermore, all acts of worship, such as prayer, zakat, etc., are forms of supplication. Sidi Shaykh also said that it is good for the servant to supplicate Allah through the Prophet ﷺ and his Shaykh.

Sidi Shaykh added that lowering oneself and exalting others is an act of the disciple out of fear of Allah, not to fulfill religious or worldly needs. It is done so that Allah may reveal to the disciple that His secrets are hidden in His creation, and the disciple may understand that all creatures are manifestations of Allah's Attributes and Names, serving as a message from Allah to him. That's why the Prophet ﷺ said: "A believer is the mirror of his brother."[71]

Sidi Shaykh stated that when confronted with unjust people, there are two ways to interpret the situation. Either the person is unjust himself, thus attracting more similar people, or it is a test from Allah. If people attack and harm a person, it will depend on his strength and persistence in facing the challenge. This test is only a temporary stage and not a permanent situation. The disciple better passes this stage in his life rather than facing it in the hereafter.

When the disciple encounters opposition from people, it is regarded as a stage in his spiritual journey towards God. It serves as a test and a challenge for him to endure some of the same difficulties faced by his Shaykh. If he remains patient and successfully passes the test, he will receive Allah's support. Sidi Shaykh then referred to the verse: "**When Allah's help comes and the victory, and you see the people embracing Allah's Way in crowds**"[72]. On the other hand, if the disciple fails the test, he becomes one of them and the devil becomes his *Wali* and enters into the cycle of evil and darkness (*da'irat al-sawu'*).

....

71   Al-Bukhari, Muhammad. *Al-Adab al-Mufrad.* #238.
72   Quran 110:1-2.

*

The four perfect women

Q: A disciple had a dream vision (*ru'ya*), where Sidi Shaykh told her that her secret is in Mariam.

Sidi Shaykh said that Ummuna Mariam, peace be upon her, is the unique woman that has been mentioned in the Quran. Allah gave her the fire or the heat of love and passion so she stayed in her spiritual seclusion with Allah in the mosque of Jerusalem.

Sidi Shaykh added that the Mosque of al-Quds is the house to all Prophets, peace be upon them. It is the house of knowledge, unlike Mecca which is the house of security and peace, whoever enters it is safe. It is a holy place where the Prophet's ascension took place. He prayed two units of prayers with all the Prophets as their imam.

Sidi Shaykh added that Ummuna Mariam, peace be upon her, was filled with love and longing for the Presence of God. The heat of love flowed from her chest and heart until reaching her womb, and God granted her a spiritual breath that cooled the heat of love and produced Sayyiduna Issa, peace be upon him. She is considered one of the four perfect women mentioned by the Prophet ﷺ, who are: Ummuna Mariam, Ummuna Khadija, Ummuna Fatima al-Zahra, and Ummuna Assiya.

Sidi Shaykh talked about the four of them and started with Ummuna Mariem, peace be upon her. He explained that she represents the image of the woman who did not marry and no man has touched her. Despite this, she guarded herself and did not follow any desires. Sidi Shaykh added that it is a message for all female disciples to safeguard themselves, especially their virginity which has become devalued nowadays.

Sidi Shaykh insisted on this point and said that it is not an extreme opinion; it is just a reality. He added that if a woman did not marry, she should protect herself and stay directed towards the *qibla*, praying just like Ummuna Mariam. Maybe Allah wants her for His *qibla* and for worship, or maybe for a greater secret. The secret was understood by Ummuna Mariam.

Sidi Shaykh then spoke about Ummuna Assiya. He mentioned that she was also a perfect woman, a believer, and a Muslim. However, her husband, pharaoh, claimed to be a god and treated her poorly. Additionally, she was unable to bear children. Despite this, she spent her life in worship of Allah and stands as an example to follow for married women.

Sidi Shaykh added that perfect women produce to the universe what the eye cannot see and the ear cannot hear. Ummuna Assiya raised Sayyiduna Musa, peace be upon him, and Ummuna Mariam gave birth to Sayyiduna Issa peace be upon him. These two Prophets represent the biggest presences (*hadarat*) in Islam, after the presence of the Prophet Muhammad ﷺ.

Then comes Ummuna Khadija, the wife of the Prophet Muhammad ﷺ. She had a large business, but she never worked in the fields or traveled with the caravans. She managed from behind the scenes, protected herself, and waited until she married the Prophet ﷺ.

Ummuna Fatima al-Zahra, blessings and peace be upon her, was the wife of Sayyiduna Ali, may Allah honor his face, the gate of the city of knowledge. Her Father was the Prophet Muhammad ﷺ. She was extremely humble and dedicated her life to serving her father, husband, and children. Despite her knowledge, she remained behind the veil, and her knowledge was not revealed until after her death when she was buried at night.

The Prophet ﷺ referred to her as the mother of her father due to her wisdom. However, when examining history, all the knowledge was attributed to Sayyiduna Ali, may Allah honor his face, as Ummuna Fatima al-Zahra was behind the veil, similar to Ummuna Khadija, the wife of the Prophet ﷺ.

*

Spending for the sake of Allah

Q: The same disciple saw in a dream vision (*ru'ya*) that she gave a gift of 1000 dinars to Sidi Shaykh. Initially, he didn't accept it, but when she insisted and suggested that he use the money to buy something for his children, he finally accepted it.

Sidi Shaykh stated that the money was accepted from the disciple as a sign that she had spent the same amount for the sake of Allah (*lillah*) in the physical realm (*mulk*). This spending was accepted by Allah, which is why the Shaykh accepted the money in the dream.

He added that giving charity, such as *sadaqah* and *nafaqah*, is a commendable deed, and he encourages disciples to do it. However, when the Shaykh requests something from a disciple, it holds a distinct significance.

Indeed, in such instances, the disciple should feel joyous because Allah has selected her among others to perform this act, which could potentially be the key to paradise for her. The request could be either material or non-material, as simple as offering a cup of water. This is why the Prophet ﷺ said: "Guard yourselves from the fire of hell even if it be with half a date."[73]

Sidi Shaykh explained that this half of the date is not for anyone but for the person to whom Allah referred in the Hadith *Qudsi* where He said: "O son of Adam, I asked you for food and you fed Me not. He will say: O Lord, and how should I feed You when You are the Lord of the worlds? He will say: Did you not know that My servant So-and-so asked you for food and you fed him not? Did you not know that had you fed him you would surely have found that with Me?"[74]

Sidi Shaykh also referenced the verse: "**Of their goods, take alms, that so thou mightest purify and sanctify them;**

....

73 *Sahih Bukhari* #1417.
74 *Sahih Muslim* #2569.

and pray on their behalf. Verily thy prayers are a source of security for them: And Allah is One Who heareth and knoweth."[75]

Sidi Shaykh continued to explain that when the righteous (*al-salihin*) and Saints (*awliya'*) wish goodness for someone, they visit his house and take something they like. If he comprehends the message, he will feel content. However, if he fails to grasp it, he will refuse saying that he needs this thing.

*

Circumambulating around the Shaykh and with the Shaykh

Q: A disciple had a dream vision in which he found himself performing circumambulation (*tawaf*) around the Shaykh, and then the Shaykh joined him. The Shaykh then advised him: "This is how you avoid temptation (*fitna*)." During the dream, the disciple also saw a woman in front of him.

In his response, Sidi Shaykh explained that circumambulating around the Shaykh is a secret, and circumambulating with the Shaykh is another different secret. Circumambulating around the Shaykh represents wayfaring (*suluk*), self-exertion (*mujahadat al-nafs*), and striving to achieve extinction (*fana'*) in the presence of the Shaykh. On the

....

75   Quran 9:103.

other hand, circumambulating with the Shaykh helps in wayfaring. It is as if the Shaykh moves from his origin, the center, to the periphery, to assist the disciple in his wayfaring.

Sidi Shaykh added that concerning temptation (*fitna*), it is a clear message for the disciple here that his temptation lies with women. To avoid it, he needs to follow the Shaykh, circumambulate around him, and do whatever pleases him. Moreover, circumambulating with him means that he will emulate him in everything he does, including his sayings and actions.

*

Conditions to practice *dhikr* of the Name Allah with the Shaykh

Q: A disciple asked if he can engage in the remembrance of the Name of Majesty "Allah" with the Shaykh during the last third of the night while watching the live video on Facebook, even though he doesn't have permission to invoke this Name.

In his answer, Sidi Shaykh granted permission to every disciple watching the live stream of Sidi Shaykh to perform *dhikr* of The Name of Majesty "Allah" under the following conditions:

- To verify that the Shaykh is present and engaged in remembrance of the Name of Majesty "Allah" in the live stream.

- To confirm that the video is live and being streamed in real-time, not a recording of a previous live video. Disciples who don't have permission to perform the remembrance of the Name of Majesty "Allah", cannot perform this remembrance following a recorded live video; it must be done in real-time.
- To ensure being in the direction of *qibla* and in a state of ritual purity.
- Regardless of what time it is in the disciple's country, he can still follow the live video and perform the remembrance with the Shaykh.

Later in the same lecture, Sidi Shaykh spoke about the night prayer (*qiyam al-layl*). He mentioned that it is recommended to pray ten units of prayer with Surah al-Ikhlas repeated ten times, each time preceded by the Basmala. Alternatively, another possibility is to recite Surah al-Ikhlas eleven times in each unit of prayer.

Lecture 21.
February 5, 2023

*

Witnessing a purple Light

Q: While practicing remembrance, a disciple witnessed
the Light in the form of a lamp. The lamp was pierced and
a purple Light was coming out of it.

Sidi Shaykh stated that the example of the Divine Light
is like a lamp in a glass. Allah did not say it was a pierced
lamp. The lamp is protected by the glass, and what one
sees is only the glass. The lamp is not a tangible object, but
rather an energy.

Sidi Shaykh made an analogy with a physical lamp. He
stated that the physical lamp is always referenced with the
form of the glass that encases it. However, the reality of this
physical lamp is the electricity and the energy, not the glass
that can be seen and touched.

Regarding the vision of Light, Sidi Shaykh said that the
glass represents the reunion of the Divine Names (*jam'iyyat
al-asma'*). Outwardly, there are indeed ninety-nine Divine

Names, but there are also Hadiths of the Prophet ﷺ in which he mentions the existence of hidden Names (*asma' ghaybiyyah*).

The color purple is associated with the Divine Name the Friend (*al-Wali*). The goal of the disciple in the vision is to focus on the center of the Light and try to draw nearer to it. However, he can never reach it, for if he were to do so, he would be burned.

*

Striving for sincerity in actions

Q: In a dream vision (*ru'ya*), a disciple saw Sidi Shaykh visiting her. While she was preparing dinner for him, an old woman appeared and stole the food, claiming it was for her.

Sidi Shaykh explained that when the Shaykh requests something from the disciple, it is not a voluntary donation or gift, but rather an obligation for the disciple. The disciple must fulfill the request and should never doubt his ability to do so, as the Shaykh's words come from a sanctified Presence (*hadra quddusiyyah*). Sidi Shaykh added that there is no room for interpretation or alteration of the order in regard to the request made by the Shaykh. The disciple must fulfill it exactly as it was given.

Sidi Shaykh further added that if the food prepared for him was taken by someone else in the dream, it is because the act was not purely for the sake of Allah (*lillah*), and there may have been other intentions from the soul (*al-nafs*) involved. That's why the disciple should strive for sincerity (*ikhlas*) in all of his actions. By doing so, he can ensure that his actions are purely for the sake of Allah and free from any selfish motives.

Sidi Shaykh then referenced a Hadith *Qudsi*: "O son of Adam, I fell ill and you visited Me not. He will say: O Lord, and how should I visit You when You are the Lord of the worlds? He will say: Did you not know that My servant So-and-so had fallen ill and you visited him not? Did you not know that had you visited him you would have found Me with him?"[76] If the disciple doesn't pay a visit to the Shaykh when it is obligatory, it means that all of his previous visits were not truly for the Shaykh but rather driven by a hidden intention in his heart. In that case, the disciple would have failed the test.

*

The importance of focusing on the center

Q: A disciple had a dream vision where she struck a young little girl on her head with a bottle only to realize she was Sidi Shaykh's daughter. The disciple was very intimidated by what she did and asked her for forgiveness. Then she found herself in the Zawiya visiting the Shaykh with fear. He told her to go and see someone specific.

....

76   *Sahih Muslim* #2569.

Sidi Shaykh explained that the Shaykh has spiritual and physical children as well as spiritual-only children. He also explained that if the disciple doesn't know how to interact with the Shaykh or put veils and barriers between him and the Shaykh, the Shaykh will do the same with him.

Sayyiduna al-Khidr, peace be upon him, instructed Sayyiduna Musa, peace be upon him, saying: **"If you follow me"**, indicating that Sayyiduna Mussa should follow only al-Khidr. However, when Sayyiduna al-Khidr discovered that Sayyiduna Musa was preoccupied with the.people on the boat, the child, and the wall, and was neglectful of him, he decided to part ways with him.

Sidi Shaykh mentioned that the disciple has always been heedless about the center, even though the *Wali* has been with him since his early age. When he finally recognized that the Shaykh is the center and came to pledge allegiance to him, he brought everything from his past and wanted to impose it. In doing so, he will never find an answer. If all the disciples, even if they number millions, were to focus only on the center, they would all reach knowledge in a blink. Instead, they are attempting to impose their own matters onto the center.

Sidi Shaykh added that the disciple should focus on the center, which is the Shaykh, and leave the past behind without bringing it along. The Shaykh should be considered as a source from which to draw, rather than a receptacle to fill with one's own matters.

Sidi Shaykh added that when the Shaykh wants to establish a veil between himself and the disciple, he sends him to other disciples every time he comes to him. That's a mercy for the disciple and at the same time a method that he chose by directing himself to other disciples and being neglectful of the center and the Imam.

*

Engaging in remembrance of the Name Allah with the Shaykh

Q: A disciple requested permission to engage in the remembrance of the Name of Majesty "Allah" with the Shaykh during the last third of the night.

Sidi Shaykh once again granted permission for all disciples to participate in *dhikr* live streamed in the last third of the night, under specific conditions outlined in the lecture from February 4th, 2023.

Sidi Shaykh said that for disciples who want to participate in *dhikr* of the Name of Majesty "Allah" with the Shaykh, it is obligatory to make sure that he is present. He added that this is for the ones who want knowledge and elevation.

Sidi Shaykh then spoke about disciples who come to the Zawiya but don't join the group in *dhikr* and prayers. He described such behavior as pride (*kibr*).

*

A kiss from the Shaykh symbolizes love

Q: A disciple had a dream vision in which he saw the Shaykh kissing him on the forehead. Then, in the exact same place where the Shaykh kissed him, he saw a bright sun, its light reaching the horizon.

Sidi Shaykh explained that a kiss symbolizes love, and a kiss on the forehead symbolizes respect and appreciation. The respect of the Shaykh to the disciple brings the disciple closer to the Prophet ﷺ.

Sidi Shaykh mentioned a story about a Shaykh who would frequently pass by a street where children played football. Each time he passed by, the children would stop their game, approach him to kiss his hand, help him carry his belongings, and ask for his *du'a*. One day, the Shaykh decided to change this situation. He took their ball and threw it away. In response, the children began to throw rocks at him. The Shaykh realized that he had been mistaken in thinking that people respected him. In reality, it was he who sought respect for himself.

Lecture 22.
February 12, 2023

*

Qawasim al-Quran

Q: A disciple asked about *qawasim al-Quran* and why they are found only in some Surahs and not in others.

Sidi Shaykh said that *qawasim al-Quran* are letters that appear at the beginning of certain Surahs. These letters can be connected or disconnected, such as in Surah al-Shura: "*Ha-Mim, 'Ayn-Sin-Qaf*"[77]. They count 14 letters if the repeated ones are removed, and 119 if they are counted individually.

....

77   Quran 42:1.

Qawasim al-Quran

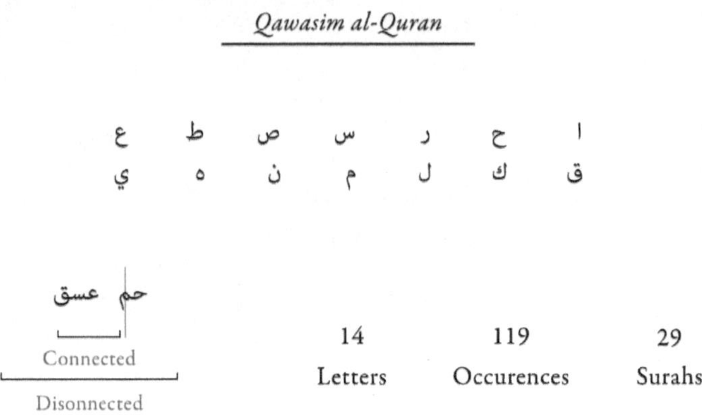

نص حكيم قاطع له سـر

A wise and conclusive text that has a secret

When these Arabic letters are arranged, they create the phrase: "A wise and conclusive text that has a secret." This secret is *al-'Itra* of *Ahl al-Bayt*, which is represented by the Dot (*al-nuqta*). Therefore, these letters indicate the secret of the Quran.

Qawasim al-Quran appeared in 29 Surahs according to the number of lunar stations or days of a month. They come in the first verse of the Surah, after the Basmala, as the Basmala is not a verse of the Surah but a verse from al-Fatiha. Sidi Shaykh referenced the Hadith of Sayyiduna Ali, may Allah honor his face: "All what is in the Quran is included in the Fatiha, and all what is in the Fatiha is included in *Bism Allah al-Rahman al-Rahim*, and all what is in *Bism Allah al-Rahman al-Rahim* is included in *Bism Allah*, and all what is in *Bism Allah* is included in the '*Ba*', and the secret of the *Ba* is the dot, and I am the Dot."

Sidi Shaykh also said that on the first page of the Quran, there is Surah al-Fatiha, and on the next page the first verses of Surah al-Baqara, from "*Alif-Lam-Mim*" to "**and it is they who will be successful**". He recommended praying the Subh prayer with these verses.

Sidi Shaykh explained further that the number of letters in these verses of Surah al-Baqara is equal to 119, the same as the number of occurrences of *qawasim al-Quran*. These verses contain the secret of the number and they inform about the secret of *qawasim al-Quran*.

Sidi Shaykh added that "*Alif-Lam-Mim*" is considered the greatest of its secrets. All of the *qawasim* are hidden in "*Alif-Lam-Mim*". Some of them are in the letter '*alif*', others are in the letter '*lam*', and some in the letter '*mim*'. In terms of numerical value, "*Alif-Lam-Mim*" equals 71. One for the '*alif*', thirty for the '*lam*', and forty for the '*mim*'. The righteous ones (*al-salihin*) said that the letter '*alif*' is the *Alif* of monotheism (*alif al-tawhid*). As for the letter '*lam*' it is for Sayyiduna Jibril, peace be upon him, and the letter '*mim*' is for the Prophet Muhammad ﷺ.

Sidi Shaykh added that *qawasim al-Quran* appeared in 29 Surahs which is equal to the number of lunar stations and days of a month as an indication that they represent the positions of the stars that carry the concealed book (*al-kitab al-maknun*). Sidi Shaykh stated that al-Fatiha and the opening verses of Surah al-Baqara are sufficient to understand the Quran if one has piety and faith.

Sidi Shaykh explained that if the Quran is likened to a wall (*sur*), the number of occurrences of *qawasim al-Quran* would correspond to the number of pillars of the wall, with 14 representing the original ones. Their secret lies within three letters: the '*alif*', the '*lam*', and the '*mim*'. The '*alif*' and the '*lam*' are used to define the '*mim*'. They are like the crystal (*zujaja*) to the lamp (*misbah*). If this wall is built, it will have the form of a center, in a ring, in a ring.

Sidi Shaykh added that those who have permission to witness this, are people of piety who really perform prayers, *zakat*, and *nafaqah*. Sidi Shaykh referred to the verse of Surah al-Baqara: "**Who believe in the unseen, establish prayer, and donate from what We have provided for them.**"[78] They establish prayer in the right way and do not just fulfill the prayer, as it is a connection and a continuous link with Allah. Sidi Shaykh added regarding *nafaqah*. He mentioned that outwardly, these people donate the *nisab* of *zakat*, but in reality, they seek any action that will purify their souls. They do so to seek the Light of Allah and to purify their souls, hearing, and sight.

Provision (*rizq*) goes beyond just money; knowledge, children, a home, all are provisions. Spending isn't restricted to money alone, it involves giving from all aspects of life, including children, spouse, time, and preaching for Islam (*da'wa*). If a person is not like that, he is not considered among the people of piety.

....

78 Quran 1:3.

Sidi Shaykh explained that Allah created four paradises. The first paradise is the mother's womb. The person spends a complete night there. In this world's time, it is nine months, but in reality, it is just one night.

Then comes the paradise of earth, its inward (*batin*) is fire but its outward is paradise. Life there is between sixty and seventy, as the Prophet ﷺ said: "The age of My *ummah* is between sixty and seventy years."[79] It is called the paradise of knowledge (*jannat al-maʿrifa*).

The next paradise is the paradise of the tomb. It is also a one-night stay there but it is unknown how much it counts in this world's time. For example, someone who died yesterday spent one night there, also Sayyiduna Adam, peace be upon him, spent one night.

Sidi Shaykh said that the last paradise is the highest Firdaus, *inshallah*, and it is eternal and the highest level in paradise. The Prophet ﷺ said: "And if you ask for paradise, then ask for the highest Firdaus."[80]

Sidi Shaykh added that just as Allah has provided the person with these paradises, he must spend from what Allah has provided for him. Therefore, when a person is filled with regret in the hereafter, he will say: "If only I could go back and give in charity." That is why *sadaqah* and *nafaqah* are a duty for the people of piety. They spend on themselves and do not wait for others, rather they spend on others. That's why *nafaqah* and spending can represent an obstacle for the

....

79 *Jamiʿ al-Tirmidhi* #2331.
80 *Jamiʿ al-Tirmidhi* #2530.

disciple in his path. The disciple achieves piety by establishing prayer, giving zakat, spending in the path of Allah, and believing in the unseen. This is difficult to achieve and that's why it is not easy to learn *qawasim al-Quran*.

Lecture 23.
February 15, 2023

*

Being with the Shaykh is higher than manifestations

Q: A disciple stated that it is getting harder for him to reflect when practicing *dhikr.*

Sidi Shaykh said that the disciple should engage in a lot of *dhikr* before starting to reflect, as reflecting without continuous *dhikr* may exceed Allah's limits. Sidi Shaykh referred to the verse: "**Who remember Allah while standing or sitting or on their sides and give thought to the creation of the heavens and the earth.**"[81] He explained that in the verse, it is evident that they engaged in *dhikr* while standing, sitting, and on their sides. Afterward, they began reflecting on the creation of the heavens and the earth.

Sidi Shaykh added that the disciple received the Light of Allah as a gift from the Shaykh, without doing anything. It is a gift from Allah and a share (*qisma*) distributed by the

....

81   Quran 3:191.

171

Shaykh to the disciple. When the disciple is doing *dhikr* of Allah with the Shaykh and the Shaykh tells him to close his eyes and engage in *dhikr* Allah, the Shaykh is teaching him his wayfaring (*suluk*) and how to behave in the presence of Allah.

If the disciple is with the Shaykh and doesn't witness the Light, his presence with the Shaykh is higher than seeing the Light and not being present with him. The disciple who is seeking manifestations (*tajalliyat*), visions, and ascension, his presence with the Shaykh is higher than manifestations, sciences, and visions. It is like someone who is sitting by a river of fresh water and asking Allah to bless him with rainwater. If one is still asking for rainwater while he is in the river, it means that he is very dull. Therefore, whoever has a living Shaykh in his time and is still searching in books and in what others said, he better take off his rosary and walk away. He is not considered among the people (*ahl*) of the Tariqa, because he is stagnant and dull and does not understand anything.

Sidi Shaykh added that the objective of the pledge of allegiance and of following the *Sunnah* of the Prophet ﷺ is to be with him or to see him in a dream or in wakefulness. If this happens to someone it will be the best thing in his life.

If one enters the mosque of the Prophet ﷺ, greets him, and the Prophet ﷺ responds to him, it is the highest blessing that can happen to someone. If someone finds himself with the Prophet ﷺ in *al-Rawda al-Sharifa* while the Prophet ﷺ is on the pulpit, would he close his eyes and try to see the Light? How dull would that be? Or if one enters *al-Rawda al-Sharifa* and finds the companions there, will he stay with them and start asking them questions or just looking at the Prophet ﷺ will satisfy him?

This is why the disciple doesn't see manifestations (*tajalli-yat*) because he doesn't exalt even the body of the source. The disciple is staying with the Shaykh and thinking of other things that he wants to achieve. Just his presence with the Shaykh should satisfy him. That's why the folk of Allah (*ahl Allah*) said that looking at the *Wali* is better than 70 years of worship.

Therefore, even though Sayyiduna Umar, God be pleased with him, had a great status, and even though the Prophet ﷺ said: "If there was a prophet after Me, it would have been Umar"[82], when Umar came to the Prophet ﷺ and said: "O Messenger of Allah, I love you" the Prophet ﷺ said: "None of you truly believes until I am more beloved to him than his wealth, his family, and himself."[83]

The disciple must honor and exalt the source of Allah's Light in order to reach it. Those who have reached haven't done so through the abundance of deeds, but rather through love and faith.

The belief in Allah and everything that comes from Him, such as angels, Prophets, and so on, is not based on seeing them and then believing in them, but rather believing in them while they are in the unseen. That is why the Prophet ﷺ said: "I long for my beloveds." The companions

....

82 *Jami' al-Tirmidhi* #3686.
83 *Sahih Bukhari* #6632.

said: "Are we not your beloveds, O Messenger of Allah?" He said to them: "My beloveds are those who believe in me but have not seen me."[84]

*

Greeting the Shaykh the proper way

Q: A disciple asked about the proper way to greet the Shaykh

Sidi Shaykh said that saying *as-salamu alaykum* is sufficient for greeting the Shaykh. As for kissing the hand of the Shaykh, it depends on the disciple's intention. However, kissing the Shaykh's head is not recommended and is considered a lack of etiquette (*adab*). It is better for the disciple to remain at the hands' level as he pledged allegiance with the hand. Sidi Shaykh referred to the Hadith: "Whoever shakes hands with Me, or shakes hands with someone who has shaken hands with Me, will enter paradise until the Day of Resurrection."

Sidi Shaykh further emphasized that kissing the foot is also not recommended, especially if the disciple hasn't acquired the science of the Names (*'ilm al-asma'*). However, there may be exceptions, such as when the disciple enters and finds the Shaykh raising his hand for *dhikr*. In such cases, the disciple can kiss the spot where the Shaykh used to place his hands on his leg.

....

84   Al-Nabulsi, Muhammad Ratib. *Riyadh al-Salihin*. Page 377.

*

The Day of Increase (*yawm al-mazid*)

Q: A disciple asked a question about the Day of Increase (*yawm al-mazid*).

Sidi Shaykh stated that the Day of Increase is a day when people who have the privilege to be present will see the face of their Lord, but it doesn't stay forever, it is just one day. It is the day of Friday for the people of paradise.

People of the Day of Increase live in paradise just like others. However, they don't remain on that day forever as it is a complete and total presence with Allah on that day, there's no eating or drinking etc.

Sidi Shaykh added that even in paradise, there exists heedlessness, which is represented by the pleasures of paradise. However, on the Day of Increase, there are no pleasures. Instead, everyone stays in a circle, according to his rank, position, or status that he worked on in his life, and he will find his place waiting for him in one of the circles

Sidi Shaykh explained that the descent of the Real (*al-Haqq*), occurs in a central position surrounded by circles: circles of Messengers, circles of Prophets, circles of militants, etc. Each circle has chairs, every chair waits for its owner. This latter is directed towards his chair directly by inspiration and guidance from Allah and stays there to look at the manifestation (*al-tajalli*) of the All-Merciful.

In this world, Allah descends in the last third of the night and says: "Is there anyone seeking forgiveness, Is there anyone in need?" It can be said that this descent (*tanazul*) is in separation (*farq*), even if a person is in a group, Allah descends to each individual and says: "Is there anyone seeking forgiveness?"[85]

[Note: In the Hadith previously mentioned, the Prophet ﷺ informs that every night, when two-third of the night is over, Allah descends to the lowest heaven.]

It is similar on the Day of Increase, but on that day, Allah descends in union (*jam'*), in the center of all the presents. Then comes the separation, where Allah speaks to each person apart and tells him: "Do you remember that dark night when you were alone with your Lord and no one else was with you, and you committed the sin that you did?" The servant replies: "Did you not forgave me O Allah?" Allah says to him: "Yes, I did. I just wanted to remind you." Then Allah reveals his face and they all get the chance to look at the All-Merciful.[86]

....

85   *Sahih Muslim* #758c.
86   *Jami' al-Tirmidhi* #2549.

Lecture 24.
February 18, 2023

*

"Choose your Imams your intercessors
on the Day of Resurrection"

Q: A disciple had a dream vision of Sidi Shaykh piloting a boat across the Nile River in Egypt, from the east side to the west side. Afterwards, the disciple saw him standing in front of a court where he said to him: "We're done, you are free to go."

Sidi Shaykh stated that according to the Prophet ﷺ, the Nile River is a river from paradise. He added that a lot of Prophets and Messengers have been in Egypt. In the past, the east of the Nile River symbolized life, agriculture, castles, and capitals of different civilizations that have been there. The west side was instead a representation of death and tombs.

Sidi Shaykh returned to interpreting the dream vision and explained that the Shaykh guided the disciple from the east to the west, from life to death, to annihilation (*fana'*). This life is a bridge; the disciple should successfully cross this

177

bridge in peace. It should be a straight path (*sirat mustaqim*) for him, as life is nothing but a *sirat*.

Sidi Shaykh added that the disciple will not traverse this bridge alone but with the Quran and Elite (*al-ʿitra*) of *Ahl al-Bayt*, as the Prophet ﷺ said: "I left in you two matters as long as you hold to them, you will not go the wrong way. The book of Allah and the Elite (*al-ʿitra*) of *Ahl al-Bayt*."[87]

The Elite (*al-ʿitra*) of *Ahl al-Bayt* is represented by Sayyiduna Ali, peace be upon him, and those who inherit his knowledge. They are the guides on this path, and they will even intercede on behalf of the disciple in the court for what he has done in his life. The Prophet ﷺ said: "Choose your imams as they are your intercessors on the Day of Resurrection."[88]

*

The importance of permission (*idhn*)

Q: In a dream vision, a disciple found himself driving a bus, while the passengers with him searched for the button to turn on the light in the bus.

Sidi Shaykh said that the disciple here became responsible (*mukallaf*), and thus, he has a duty to preach the message of

....

87 *Jami' al-Tirmidhi* #3788.

88 Al-Zurqani, Muhammad. *Sharh al-Zurqani ʿAla Muwatta' Imam Malik*. Vol. 1, "Your Imams are your intercessors"; Al-Bayhaqi, Abu Bakr. *Al-Sunan al-Kubra*. Vol. 1, Page 128, "Make your Imams from amongst your best".

the path of Allah through *da'wa*. The Prophet ﷺ said in a Hadith: "Convey from me; even if only one verse."[89] In another Hadith, he ﷺ said: "The best among you are those who learn the Quran and teach it."[90] Thus, the disciple shouldn't conceal what he has learned but should help others in the same bus with him. *Da'wa* requires the Light because someone who doesn't have the Light essentially has nothing. He who has no Light has nothing. The one who lacks Light possesses neither prayer, nor knowledge, nor anything. Therefore, one must seek the Light of Allah to attain the presence of the Prophet ﷺ and the presence of the Almighty.

Sidi Shaykh added that in order to have the Light of Allah it is mandatory to have permission (*idhn*). That's why even though the people in the bus followed the disciple, they are not considered among the people of Light (*ahl al-Nur*) because they don't have permission. That's why they are searching for the button to turn on the Light.

Sidi Shaykh told the story of someone who sought treatment from an Islamic spiritual healer (*raqi*) who was not from the Tariqa Karkariya. The healer prescribed to him the litany (*al-wird*) of the Tariqa and advised him to practice it as a treatment. This person started to see Sidi Shaykh in the spiritual realm, but in the physical realm, he became unstable. This is because he doesn't have permission (*ijaza*).

For this reason, the disciple should give great importance to permission (*idhn*) without interpreting the words of the

....

89 *Jami' al-Tirmidhi* #446.
90 *Sahih Bukhari* #5027.

Shaykh. When the Shaykh grants permission for something, it is very clear. Sidi Shaykh further explained that asking for permission is not considered permission, as when the Shaykh wants a disciple to do something, he will grant permission even before the disciple asks. For example, one cannot go to the mosque and ask for the call to prayer of Duhr. Instead, he should wait for the call to prayer and pray in time.

*

Serving others (*khidma*)

Q: Serving others (*khidma*).

Later in the lecture, Sidi Shaykh spoke about serving others. He referenced the Hadith of the Prophet ﷺ: "The leader of people is their servant."[91] He also said that by serving others, a person enters into the heart. For example, a person's name may be forgotten, but he can still be remembered by his actions.

Allah said in a Hadith *Qudsi*: "And My Servant continues to draw near to Me with supererogatory deeds until I Love him."[92] These supererogatory deeds (*nawafil*) are not about speaking, as speaking cannot lead the disciple to knowledge. Knowledge is attained by drawing near to Allah

....

91   Al-'Ajluni, Isma'il bin Muhammad. *Kachf al-Khafa'*. Vol.1, #1515; al-Khatib al-Tabrizi, Muahammad Ibn 'Abdullah. *Mishkat al-Masabih*. #3925.
92   *Sahih Bukhari* #6502.

through actions. These actions are not even obligations, but rather supererogatory. Therefore, when the disciple remains stagnant (*jamid*), his reed cannot be lit. Allah created both stillness (*sukun*) and movement. The first thing created by Allah was stillness, yet this stillness did not know Allah until Allah looked at it, and it moved with joy. It was then that knowledge was realized. Thus, knowledge is realized through actions, not by collecting information or reading thousands of books. By serving others, the disciple gets love in his heart. Love is not about visions; love burns everything other than Allah.

Sidi Shaykh added that Allah loves the person who serves; that's why the Prophet ﷺ described work as worship (*'ibadah*). This work should be for the sake of Allah (*lillah*) and should be continuous. Even if it is not big, it should be continuous. This is reflected in the phrase "continues to draw near to Me" found in the Hadith *Qudsi*.

*

Interacting with people after repentance

Q: A disciple mentioned that in the past, he was engaged in sinful behavior and now experiences intrusive thoughts from that time. Furthermore, people in his circle are tempting him to return to his past actions.

Sidi Shaykh said that disciples who joined the Tariqa after a past of sinful behavior and then they become knowers of God (*'arifin billah*), experience a significant difference in their lives. However, they will inevitably face tests (*imtihanat*), particularly after the spiritual seclusion (*kholwa*), as they will be confronted with their past because they have not yet completed their repentance.

Repentance is achieved by ceasing the acts committed in the past and by making amends for the harm caused to others. Even if a person did not steal from someone, he still committed sins with him. Repairing the harm caused to others includes declaring repentance and performing good deeds with the same person with whom one has committed sins.

Sidi Shaykh outlined three potential scenarios. If the disciple is strong and belongs to the top category, then all members of his circle will follow him. If the disciple is average, his circle will not follow him, but he will remain steadfast on the path of Allah. However, if the disciple is weak, he will follow his circle and revert to his past actions.

This is exemplified, for instance, in the case of the wife. The wife mirrors the reality of her husband; if he is righteous (*salih*), she will emulate his behavior, and if he is not, she will also adopt his ways. Therefore, the husband should never blame his wife.

There may be exceptions in some cases, like in the case of Sayyiduna Lut, peace be upon him. He did not divorce his wife, but was patient with her. Divorce should not be seen as a solution. The disciple should realize the importance of the verse: "**And enjoin prayer upon your family and be steadfast therein.**"[93]

Sidi Shaykh added that there are disciples who complain that their wives do not love the Shaykh. In fact, it is because of the husband, as the disciple is the ambassador of the Divine Light. Everyone loves worship (*'ibadah*) and *dhikr*, even though the person is not in the Tariqa. Hence, the reason the wife hates the Zawiya or the Tariqa is because of the husband.

*

Witnessing the Light during the sacred dance (*hadra*)

Q: A disciple had a vision of Light while practicing the sacred dance (*al-hadra*) where she saw the Light in a spherical shape sending rings of Light in her direction.

Sidi Shaykh explained that the main objective of the disciple is not just to see the shining star (*al-kawkab al-durri*), but to draw closer to it. This is where the rings of Light play a crucial role, as they are sent from the shining star to the disciple to purify his heart, hearing, sight, and even the structure of his body.

Therefore, the right way for the disciple to deal with these waves of Light is to strive to maintain a state of presence with the Light of Allah, and that's why this purification is

....

93 Quran 20:132.

to be performed twice a day: Once after the Subh prayer and once after the Maghrib prayer.

The righteous ones (*al-salihin*) mentioned the importance of this state of presence at least twice a day. One might say that once a day is enough. If it was the case then why would one pray five prayers a day? In reality, the integrity of the body, the intellect, the heart, and the soul requires five prayers a day.

Sidi Shaykh added that the rings of Light here can be likened to magnets that elevate the disciple from a lower to a higher state.

Lecture 25.
February 20, 2023

*

The All-Merciful (*al-Rahman*)
and the Ever-Merciful (*al-Rahim*)

Q: In this part of the lecture Sidi Shaykh spoke about the fifth verse of Surah Taha: **"The All-Merciful, established on the Throne"**[94].

Sidi Shaykh explained that The Throne is the highest, most precious, and closest creature to the Creator. This means that the greatness of the Throne is incomparable to any other creature's greatness. Therefore, the descent (*al-tanazul*) of the Name "the All-Merciful" (*al-Rahman*), from the Name of Majesty "Allah" that refers to the Essence, is His establishment (*istiwa'*) on the Throne.

Sidi Shaykh added that the Name "the All-Merciful" (*al-Rahman*) encompasses all creatures. **"The All-Merciful, established on the Throne"** means that everything below

....

94 Quran 20:5.

the Throne is under the dominion of the All-Merciful. Therefore, the All-Merciful is the leader and commander of all these entities. Allah says in the Quran: "**And My mercy encompasses all things.**"[95] So, this mercy encompasses all things, whether humans know it, comprehend it, or not, and in all realms: in the physical realm, spiritual realm, and the realm of invincibility.

In contrast to the Name "the All-Merciful", the Name "the Ever-Merciful" (*al-Rahim*) is specific to believers, as Allah says: "**And to the believers is kind and merciful (*rahim*).**"[96]. Its exclusivity or its role is with believers and not with other entities. As for the All-Merciful, it has the widest inclusivity and a broader scope, englobing all the creation. So, if one wants to differentiate, the throne-status (*'arshiyyah*) of the All-Merciful is different from the throne-status of the Ever-Merciful. The dominion of the All-Merciful is for all entities, and the dominion of the Ever-Merciful is for believers.

*

Witnessing a Divine Name written in Light

Q: In a direct vision of Light, a disciple witnessed the Name of Allah "the Overseer" (*al-Muhaymin*).

....

95   Quran 7:156.
96   Quran 9:128.

In his answer, Sidi Shaykh said that when one of Allah's Names is written in letters for the disciple, he should focus on the source of the Name. In this case, it is the letter 'ha' of the Name "the Overseer" (*al-Muhaymin*). He should try to concentrate and exalt it as much as possible until it changes from the written (*al-mastur*) to the numbered (*al-marqum*). At that point, the Light of the Name is manifested to the disciple, as the attribute of Light of the Name is higher than the Name itself.

By visualizing the Name written in letters, the disciple realizes that the Name is reflected on his heart as if it is a gate upon which he can work. However, the way to enter the gate is by focusing on the letter 'ha' and swimming in the beauty of the Name, which is the Overseer (*al-Muhaymin*). This swimming is similar to swimming in the Name "Allah", as it is the same method with which the disciple swims in the Name of Majesty "Allah", which encompasses all the Names. The same method is used with all the other Names. However, in the case of other Names, the disciple should know the letter on which he should focus. It is not just the middle of the Name, but a specific letter, just like his focus on the 'ha' in the Name "Allah".

The letter 'ha' in the Name of Majesty "Allah" comes at the end of the Name, while in the Name "the Overseer" (*al-Muhaymin*), it is positioned in the middle of the Name. The disciple focuses on the letter 'ha' until Allah opens this gateway for him if he has acceptance (*qabul*) and permission (*idhn*) in that. Then, he will swim in the spiritual realm of the Name "the Overseer".

Sidi Shaykh finished by stating that there isn't much to say about the manifestation of a Divine Name, such as the All-Merciful or the Overseer, in letters, besides the fact that it is a manifestation (*tajalli*) of the Name. If the Name is manifested to the disciple, that means that he became closer to the Name and if he wants to work on this Name, he should focus on its throne-status (*'arshiyyah*), as it serves as the gateway to the Name. In this case, it is represented by the letter 'ha'. Then, the characteristics of this Name and the knowledge it contains appear to the disciple according to what Allah intended for him.

*

The pledge of allegiance (*al-bay'ah*)

Q: The pledge of allegiance (*al-bay'ah*).

Later in the lecture, Sidi Shaykh spoke about the pledge of allegiance (*al-bay'ah*). He explained that pledging allegiance to the Shaykh is a commitment from the disciple to sell himself and his desires to the Shaykh.
[Note: In Arabic, the words "pledge of allegiance" (*bay'ah*) and "to sell" (*ba'a*) share the same root which is (*baya'a*). The former is a derived noun, while the latter is a verb.]
Sidi Shaykh added that the folk of Allah (*ahl Allah*) said that the disciple should be like a dead person with his washer when he is with his Shaykh. If the disciple applies

this approach, he refrains from engaging in *dhikr* or any other daily activities without first seeking permission from the Shaykh.

In Surah al-Kahf, Sayyiduna Musa, peace be upon him, was not following Sayyiduna al-Khidr, peace be upon him, only in the litany but in all kinds of acts such as smashing the boat, killing the child, etc. It is not the Shaykh's role to tell the disciple how to follow him. The Shaykh will do what he has to do, and the disciple should follow.

Sidi Shaykh emphasized that following the Shaykh doesn't mean copying whether the Shaykh sits or stands. The disciple should do what the Shaykh wants and avoid what the Shaykh forbids, even if the disciple believes that the act would please Allah. If an act does not please the Shaykh, then there must be something in it that does not please Allah. This is because the Shaykh is the gate to the Prophet ﷺ, and the Prophet ﷺ is the gate to Allah.

Through his interaction and constant presence with the Shaykh, the disciple learns what the Shaykh likes and dislikes without needing to ask. When the disciple does what the Shaykh likes, the gate is opened for him. However, in the other case, even if he prays all day long, he won't be able to gain anything more than reward and blessing, and he won't be able to be in the heart of the Shaykh.

Sidi Shaykh gave examples of the foundations of the Tariqa like the patched cloak (*al-muraqa'a*), the rosary (*al-subha*), and the spiritual wandering (*al-siyaha*). He explained that the Shaykh did not choose these foundations randomly, but rather because they are things that please him. The disciple should perform them, master them, and put in effort to perfect them because since the Shaykh has set them, they please him. If the Shaykh is pleased with preaching for the path of Allah and doing *da'wa,* and he talks about it frequently, then the disciple should engage in such activity to please his Shaykh. Moreover, if there is a specific place where the Shaykh does not want the disciple to be, then the disciple should not go there and should not ask for permission. The Shaykh will tell him to go, but this going is a separation, similar to the separation between Sayyiduna Musa and Sayyiduna al-Khidr, peace be upon them.

Sidi Shaykh also spoke about attending the lectures and reading the books and poems of the Shaykh. He said that they strengthen the presence (*hudur*) of the disciple. Even if the disciple has already memorized them, he should revisit them, as he may have memorized them without fully understanding their meanings.

Lecture 26.
March, 2023

*

**"When the sky splits apart,
and it becomes a rose, like paint."**

Q: A disciple had a direct vision (*mushahada*) in his spiritual seclusion (*kholwa*) in which he witnessed a rose and at its end it emitted a purple Light.

Sidi Shaykh stated that Allah included everything in the Quran, but the result or meaning of each verse remains as if it is a secret. The disciple should read attentively and comprehend the verse until he grasps the hidden meaning. Otherwise, he is described with the verse: **"like a donkey which carries huge tomes"**[97]. Sidi Shaykh added that it is like a mathematical equation, if a person doesn't understand it, he will never get the correct result. If the disciple is habituated to getting the answer from the Shaykh without understanding, he will never learn because he never tasted and experienced this reality.

....

97   Quran 62:5.

Sidi Shaykh then referred to verses 37 through 39 of Surah al-Rahman: "**When the sky splits apart, and it becomes a rose, like paint. So which of your Lord's marvels will you deny? On that day, no human and no jinn will be asked about his sin.**"[98] He explained that the rose is not a physical object that will split apart into two parts. In reality, the intended meaning here is that heaven will split and manifest its reality and what is hidden behind it. When heaven becomes like a rose for the person who is near it at that moment, he will not be held accountable for his sins. In this case, Allah has manifested on him with the Name "the Forgiving" (*al-Ghafur*). This person will not be asked about his sins from the past and the future, because the time has stopped for him.

Sidi Shaykh added that as soon as a person reaches the splitting of the first heaven, he stops time and space for himself because time and space must inevitably produce either good deeds (*hasanat*) or bad deeds (*sayyi'at*). He becomes non-existent at that moment.

Sidi Shaykh said about the purple Light emitted by the rose that filled all the space, that at a certain level, everything disappears for the disciple, including the rose, the heaven, and all the stations that he passed by. The purple light represents the Name "the Friend" (*al-Wali*), so when everything disappeared, only the Light of the Divine Names remained. The Name that combines all the Names is the Name of Majesty "Allah", which means that only the Light of Allah remained.

....

98   Quran 55:37-39.

Sidi Shaykh added that the disciple should work on the allusions (*isharat*) that he receives from Allah. If he really intends to be a disciple, he is required to work on the allusions he receives, as well as the allusions received by his brothers in the path of Allah. If he doesn't work on that, he is not considered a disciple, he is just pretending. The allusions and messages are not just to talk about every now and then, but to work on them. For example, if someone receives a message from his father or his wife saying: "I want you to come to me right now", the objective is not just to read the message, but to apply it. It is the same for the disciple with the messages he receives from Allah. It is the same with the Quran. People read it and complete it every month, but they don't apply any of it. Some may put in more effort and memorize it, but have they applied any of it? The response is No.

Sidi Shaykh said that everyone in this world has the motivation to search for the truth (*haqiqa*) within himself. At least once in his life, he may have asked himself: "Who am I? Why do I exist, and what is my role in this life?" This is the natural disposition of all human beings, not only Muslims. Everyone wants to know the truth. It is just the level of aspiration (*himma*) that differs from one person to another. Some people are immersed in their insouciance and forget about the truth, while others are occasionally motivated by Allah to seek the truth. Every person has opportunities in his life to know the truth, and he must take advantage of them, or else he will miss out.

Sidi Shaykh used the example of the disciple who asked the question. He said that before converting to Islam and before joining the Tariqa, he searched and asked for the truth, and he was guided to meet the *Wali* and then entered the spiritual seclusion.

*

The spiritual seclusion (*al-kholwa*)

Q: The spiritual seclusion (*al-kholwa*).

Sidi Shaykh spoke about the spiritual seclusion (*al-kholwa*) in the next part of the lecture. He explained that the spiritual seclusion (*al-kholwa*) is so named because the person who enters it abandons all vices and adopts the Attributes of Allah, the Almighty. It is a gateway for the person to completely detach from his past and from the physical world, and to approach death, the small death, when entering the presence of Allah. Even if paradise were offered to him, he would refuse it because he seeks only the truth.

Thus, if the disciple truly desired to know the truth in the past, Allah responded to him by showing him the way through the Shaykh. The Shaykh is the spiritual seclusion, and the spiritual seclusion is the Shaykh. As Sayyiduna Ali, peace be upon him said: "I am the Dot" meaning that there is no separation between the Shaykh and the spiritual seclusion.

In the spiritual seclusion, nothing is accepted besides the Name of Majesty "Allah". Sidi Shaykh said that prayer is the pillar of the religion, which is why the Shaykh orders disciples to do it in the spiritual seclusion. However, fasting in *kholwa*, for example, is not like fasting on other days. It is fasting on everything besides Allah. Even The Shaykh that the disciple follows in acts, sayings, and everything he does, left and said to him to only say: "Allah".

Sidi Shaykh added that even directions are removed. The disciple is in the center of the piece, with nothing on his right, left, in front of him, or behind him. The only direction that remains is beneath him, which is also removed during *dhikr*. All the practices and efforts the disciple previously relied on to draw near to Allah, including supererogatory deeds, are removed. This is to tell him that he has only one gate to reach, which is the gate to Allah.

Sidi Shaykh added that secrets and the truth are reached in that way. Even if the Shaykh removes his clothes and gives them to the disciple or gives him a part of his body, the disciple won't reach the truth. The wayfaring (*suluk*), the path, is not an obligation or with force, but with love and extinction (*fana'*) in the Shaykh. For example, when Sayyiduna Ibrahim, peace be upon him, was ordered to sacrifice his son, Sayyiduna Ismail, peace be upon him, he didn't do so with force, but Sayyiduna Ismail agreed with love.

Sidi Shaykh said that every message sent by Allah to the disciple in the spiritual seclusion is to tell him only one thing: "My servant so and so is my *Wali*." The disciple who doesn't understand a vision in the spiritual seclusion, the reason is that he eliminated the *Wali* who admitted him there.

Sidi Shaykh also said that the disciple should have a lot of magnification (*ta'dhim*) to the Shaykh because without him the disciple won't have any vision or knowledge even if he stays in a *kholwa* for ten years.

Lecture 27.
March 4, 2023

*

The reality of the pyramids

Q: A disciple had a direct vision (*mushahada*) of Light in which he witnessed a circle in which there are ten triangles connected in the center of the circle. In each triangle, there are unreadable words. In one of the triangles, the disciple could read the Arabic word (*fass*) which translates to a bezel.

Sidi Shaykh started his answer by referring to the Hadith of the Prophet ﷺ: "I am the first among Prophets and the last of them."[99] So Sayyiduna Muhammad ﷺ is the beginning and the end. He is considered the bezel of the ring (*fass al-khatam*), and the value of the ring is in its bezel.

Sidi Shaykh added about the disciple's vision that the circle is a niche (*mishkat*) in which there is a triangle. The triangle holds a significant value, not only in the Tariqa,

....

99   Al-Ghazali, Abu Hamid. *Ma'arij al-Qudus Fi Madarij Ma'rifat al-Nafs*. Page iii.

197

as it represents the Basmala. Sidi Shaykh explained that in the Basmala there are three Divine Names: Allah in *Bism Allah*, the All-Merciful (*al-Rahman*), and the Ever-Merciful (*al-Rahim*). Additionally, in the Basmala three letters have dots: the letter '*ba*', the letter '*nun*', and the letter '*ya*'. If they are gathered together, they form a triangle or a pyramid. This triangle represents the numbered *Basmala* (*al-basmala bil-marqum*).

Sidi Shaykh also spoke about pyramids in Egypt. He said that there are three main pyramids in Egypt and they aren't randomly built. They represent secrets of the beginning of something just like the secrets contained by the Basmala at the beginning of a Surah.

Sidi Shaykh mentioned that he previously visited the pyramids and that he is talking out of direct experience not based on TV or internet information. He added that there are no corpses or tombs in the pyramids but passages that lead to a room. This room does not contain any messages or symbols about the person who lived there. In contrast, in the Valley of the Kings, there are tombs and drawings on the walls that indicate the nature of the civilization that lived there. Unlike the pyramids, which lack such elements, there is only a dark room that does not receive sunlight. It remained like an enigma for all humanity. There are three main pyramids. If likened to dots, they will be like a Basmala in a desert (*fala*).

Some astronomers said that these pyramids are linked to specific planets and galaxies. Sidi Shaykh said that they aren't totally wrong. In fact, these pyramids were not built randomly like some geometric shapes in the desert. The method of construction of these pyramids caused a lot of confusion. How could a human being, whose height does not exceed two meters, build pyramids at such heights?

In reality, the pharaohs did not build the pyramids. How could a ruler or a governor like pharaoh build the pyramids without inscribing his name or including drawings that indicate who built the pyramids, just like he did in the tombs? These pyramids are like the beginning of the Surah of Egypt, or the beginning of a civilization. As if they represent the Basmala to a Surah. Pharaoh did not build the pyramids, rather people who have esoteric knowledge did, as they know the meaning of the Basmala. They are built on sand as if they are a line of sand. The first to use geomancy (*'ilm khat al-raml*) is Sayyiduna Idriss, peace be upon him. These pyramids were built in the era of Sayyiduna Idriss, peace be upon Him, the era of the nation of Ad (*qawm 'ad*), or before that.

At that time, people lived until 900 years, and their height reached 40 meters. With such height, men can build pyramids just like houses are built nowadays. Sidi Shaykh added that the pyramids were built to hold secrets or serve as an observatory to study and observe phenomena happening in the sky.

Sidi Shaykh gave an example to explain further. He said that if a satellite is deployed in an orbit today, would it be to bury a king? No, it would be for scientific reasons. It is the same for the pyramids. If humans search for hundreds of years, they will never find a body, a mummy, or bones.

These pyramids are secrets. Even if they imagine that they will find these secrets in books and documents there, they are mistaken. The pyramids themselves, their construction, and their placement, are a secret in themselves.

Sidi Shaykh said that all mercies, everything that has degrees (*darajat*), energies, and sciences descend from the higher to the lower, from top to bottom. That's why the Prophet ﷺ described the Quran as a luminous cord extended from the heaven to the earth. If this Hadith were to be applied, a vessel would be placed to receive this extension and this power descending from heaven to earth. Some have understood this Hadith in another language, the language of the spirit. They perceive this cord of Light extended from the heaven to the earth and get knowledge from it.

Sidi Shaykh referred to the verse: "**A servant of Ours, to whom We had granted mercy from Us and enlightened with knowledge of Our Own**"[100]. Sidi Shaykh explained that knowledge here is that bright shining Light descending from the higher to the lower. This servant read it in the language of Light and ascended in it. This is what is known as knowledge directly from Allah (*'ilm laduni*), unlike those who derive rules from what they read in the written book (*al-mastur*). As for the cord extended from the heaven to the earth, it is called the numbered book (*al-marqum*), and the one that remains in the positions of the stars as stored energy is called the concealed book (*al-maknun*). Sidi Shaykh referred to verses 75 through 77

....

100 Quran 18:65.

in Surah al-Waqi'a: "**So I do swear by the positions of the stars and this, if only you knew, is indeed a great oath that this is truly a noble Quran.**"[101] It means that in the positions of the stars, there is a Quran where there are 114 Basmala, but it is not written down, rather it is concealed (*maknun*) and it cannot be touched or approached except by people of purity (*tahara*).

That's what the people of purity did, they built an observatory, just like the Shaykh built a Zawiya and another built a mosque to honor the rituals of Allah (*sha'air Allah*). Sidi Shaykh also referred to Sayyiduna Ibrahim, peace be upon him, who built the house of Allah that all Muslims pilgrimage to it. All these are as if the rituals of Allah were built in his physical realm by revelation to his servants. This is considered a higher science (*'ilm 'ulwi*), not a burial ground for Ramesses or Khufu, as people think.

Sidi Shaykh returned to the disciple's vision and said that the ten triangles seen by the disciple represent the ten lectures, and its bezel (*fass*), is the veil of Prophet Muhammad ﷺ, the greatest veil (*al-hijab al-a'dham*). When this greatest veil is revealed or reached, the greatest example is reached with all of its secrets. Sidi Shaykh added that all of this is an introduction to understanding the importance of the three dots. Every Surah starts with three dots, except Surah al-Tawba which starts with one dot, the dot of the letter '*ba*' in the word *bara'a* in the first verse of the Surah

....

101 Quran 56:75-77.

Sidi Shaykh stated that talking about Egypt should not refer to pharaohs but rather to the civilizations of Prophets and Messengers who lived in this country, such as Sayyiduna Musa and Sayyiduna Yusuf, peace be upon them.

*

The location of the stars

Q: In this part of the lecture, Sidi Shaykh first spoke about the example of the Divine Light.

Sidi Shaykh said that the example of the Divine Light is composed of the niche (*al-mishkat*), the glass (*al-zujaja*), the lamp (*al-misbah*), and the shining star (*al-kawkab al-durri*). The union of the glass and the lamp is the shining star, and the lamp is the highest example of the four. The niche is considered the container of the lamp, in which the secrets and sciences of the lamp are found.

In Surah al-Waqi'a verses 75 through 77 Allah says: **"So I do swear by the positions of the stars and this, if only you knew, is indeed a great oath that this is truly a noble Quran."**[102] Sidi Shaykh explained that Allah is not talking about the star itself, but rather its location. The location of the star contains the knowledge and the science of the Quran. The star itself is considered to be the secret of the Quran while its location is the knowledge.

....

102 Quran 56:75-77.

Sidi Shaykh referred to verses 1 through 3 in Surah al-Najm: **"By the star when it sets, your companion has neither strayed nor erred; nor does he speak out of caprice."**[103] The star descended upon the Prophet ﷺ, and so he became the owner of the star. Everything that was manifested by the location of the star is considered as Quran. That is why the *Sunnah* of Prophet Muhammad ﷺ is considered Quran. Although some may deny this reality, the actions and sayings of the Prophet ﷺ are all Quran as they provide a living explanation of the Quran. That's why, when asked about the Prophet ﷺ, Ummuna Aisha peace be upon her, said: "He was a walking Quran."[104]

Sidi Shaykh added that when one of the companions meets the Prophet ﷺ, he receives a portion of this science from him, and what he receives one day is different from what he receives another day. For 23 years, every day a companion receives a different science or knowledge from the Prophet's ﷺ *Sunnah*, either from his verbal *Sunnah* (*sunnah qawliyyah*), practical *Sunnah* (*sunna fi'liyyah*), or declarative *Sunnah* (*sunna taqririyyah*).

Sidi Shaykh also spoke about companionship (*suhba*) and said that if a disciple claims to have a companion, he must prove what he received from him. If he received nothing, it means that his companion is empty and does not possess a star. Sidi Shaykh said that one should be a good companion to others, even if he does not have anything

....

103 Quran 53:1-3.
104 Al-Bukhari, Muhammad. *Al-Adab al-Mufrad.* #308.

to give, at the very least, he should smile in the face of his brother because smiling in the face of a brother is a charity.

That's why the Prophet ﷺ said: "My Companions are like the stars, whichever of them you follow you will be rightly guided."[105] That means that the Companions of the Prophet ﷺ are righteous, they are a source of guidance, blessing, and elevation.

*

The greatest *du'a* from the Shaykh

Q: A disciple saw in a dream vision that it was raining outside and she opened the windows of the Zawiya to let the rain in. After that, she saw Sidi Shaykh and his wife and he passed one hand on her face and heart, and placed his other hand on her head, and made *du'a* for her with Surah al-Ikhlas.

Sidi Shaykh said that the Hand of the Shaykh, of the *Wali*, is different from normal people's hand and this is proved by the Hadith *Qudsi* of the *Wali*: "And My Servant continues to draw near to Me with supererogatory deeds until I Love him. When I Love him, I become his hearing with which He hears, and his sight with which He sees, and his hand with which He strikes, and his foot with which

....

105 Al-Suyuti, Jalal al-Din. *Takhrij Ahadith al-Shifa*. Page, 193.

He walks."[106] Also, the Prophet ﷺ said in another Hadith: "Whoever shakes hands with Me, or shakes hands with someone who has shaken hands with Me, will enter paradise until the Day of Resurrection." It means that getting closer to the Prophet ﷺ or to someone close to him ﷺ is considered sanctification and purification (*tahara*). This is also proved in verse 33 of Surah al-Ahzab: "**God only desires to remove defilement from you, O People of the House, and to purify you completely.**"[107] That means that drawing near to *Ahl al-Bayt* is purification. The disciple should not imagine that he is doing a favor for the Shaykh or his Family. If he does something, it is for himself, not for others. The goodness benefits him.

Sidi Shaykh added that the *Ahl al-Bayt* of the Prophet ﷺ are purity, no one can deny this because Allah said it in the Quran. If someone claims to be from them, the people of purity, He needs to prove it with piety as the Prophet ﷺ said: "I am the grandfather of all pious"[108], and this is difficult to prove.

Sidi Shaykh explained that this distinction exists in everything, just as Allah favored the heaven over the earth. Both were created from the Light of Allah, but he made the heaven different from the earth, he elevated it and when it splits open for someone, Allah forgives all of his sins,

....

106 *Sahih Bukhari* #6502.
107 Quran 33:33.
108 Al-ʾAjluni, Ismaʿil. *Kachf al-Khafaʾ*. Vol.1, #615.

both past and future. In contrast, if the earth splits open for someone, that is considered a disaster, not an elevation.

Sidi Shaykh added that everything that descends from above is considered beneficial, especially rain (*al-ghayth*), which is considered as recently created by its Lord (*qaribat al-'ahd bi-rabbiha*). The Prophet ﷺ used to remove his turban from his head each time it rained and would make *du'a*. Allah says in the Quran Surah al-Nahl verse 65: "**And God sends down water from the sky, and thereby revives the earth after its death.**"[109] Sidi Shaykh explained that just as water gives life to the earth after its death, it also gives life to the person as it is pure. There is a Hadith where the Prophet ﷺ said: "O Allah, purify me with snow and hail and cold water."[110] Snow, hail, and cold water all come from above so they are pure. If they reach a person he must put in his intention (*niyyah*) that they are a purification for him.

Sidi Shaykh interpreted the final part of the dream where the female disciple saw him making *du'a* for her. He said that Surah al-Ikhlas represents monotheism (*al-tawhid*), and if the Shaykh makes *du'a* for someone to be among the people of monotheism (*al-muwahidin*), that is the greatest *du'a*. Because a *du'a* from the Shaykh for sustenance and relief from hardships, etc., is insignificant compared to a *du'a* that the person be faithful and among the people of monotheism. It is evident in the Hadith of the Prophet ﷺ: "The best of what I and the Prophets before Me have said,

....

109 Quran 16:65.
110 Al-Nasa'i, Ahmad. *Sunan al-Nasa'i.* #402.

is: There is no god but Allah."[111] No matter how much a person suffers from hardship in his life, the ultimate end is always the most important.

Sidi Shaykh also spoke about the importance of prayer. He explained how it is a *Sunnah* to give *adhan* in the ear of a newborn and Iqama in the other ear to tell him that the duration of his life is the same time as the duration between the *adhan* and the Iqama and to inform him about the importance of prayer, which is the pillar of religion. His entire existence is just for prayer (*salat*), meaning it is just to be in a continuous connection (*silah mawsulah*) with Allah.

At the end of his response to this question, Sidi Shaykh spoke about the fact that this earth is a paradise and explained the difference between the four paradises: the paradise of the mother's womb also called the paradise of pure meanings (*al-ma'ani*). The paradise of the earth, also called the paradise of receptacles (*al-awani*) or the paradise of actions (*al-af'al*). The paradise of the tomb as the tomb is a garden of paradise for people of faith. And finally, the eternal paradise (*jannat al-khuld*).

....

111 Ibn Anas, Imam Malik. *Muwatta' Imam Malik. Book 15, #504.*

Lecture 28.
March 17, 2023

*

How to behave with fellow disciples

Q: A lecture given by Sidi Shaykh before traveling to Saudi Arabia for Umrah.

Sidi Shaykh said that whoever isolates himself from others, under the pretext that others represent a source of harm to him or that he himself is a source of harm to others is considered a weak believer. A strong believer, on the other hand, is always in a state of monotheism (*tawhid*), meaning that he affirms the Oneness of Allah during times of temptation (*fitna*). He is always in presence and *dhikr* in all situations, not only when he is isolated during the spiritual seclusion (*kholwa*) and when does not interact with his brothers.

This type of solitary behavior directly contradicts the Hadith of The Prophet ﷺ where he said: "People who love each other with the Light of Allah."[112] This behavior is not of someone who is from the people of love. Love is not just words. If someone loves Allah, he must show that his heart is a throne for Allah. If he loves the Prophet ﷺ, he must show that his heart is a garden of the Prophet ﷺ. And if he loves the believers, he must prove that he is a mirror to his believing brother.

Sidi Shaykh added that the disciple should not think that all other disciples are angels. He should not say that this disciple should not be this way or the other should not be that way, etc. The disciple should behave as an ideal disciple. When he meets his brother, he should not look at him in a bad way. At the very least he should smile, as smiling in the face of his brother is a charity.

Also, a disciple should not project onto his brother his personal sadness which he carries with him from his wife, his work, or his business that he lost. At the bare minimum, he should perform acts of kindness, such as smiling, treating others well, and saying good words, until Allah removes his afflictions and suffering with this charity that he pushed himself to do even though he did not have the energy to do it.

Sidi Shaykh explained further that a disciple may be experiencing a lot of sadness. He may be struggling financially and tired, but he must push himself and show that he is in a good situation and does not need any help. This is how a Sufi is; he shows purity, mercy, and love. He does not hide

....

112 Al-Sijistani, Abu Dawud. *Sunan Abi Dawud*. #3527.

purity and love and shows sadness, poverty, and weakness. The disciple should talk about the blessings from Allah so that these blessings may get multiplied by Allah instead of projecting his problems onto others which only serves to block him further. This is how the disciple should behave in this sacred month of Ramadan with his brothers from among the fellow disciples and with all creatures of Allah.

Sidi Shaykh added that wearing the patched cloak (*al-muraqaʿa*) and wandering is a way for the disciple to show himself and not hide. In this way, he is leaving his isolation and showing himself to the people around him. Maybe someone will insult him with words, but as his mirror, he reflects back with patience and shows him good manners. But if he is going to wear the patched cloak (*al-muraqaʿa*) and cause chaos among people like some raging bull, then it is better to control himself and stay at home.

Sidi Shaykh added that if one is struggling financially, he should show others that he is rich. Allah will sustain him. On the other hand, the more one shows his poverty to others, the poorer he will become. But if he hides his poverty and shows his richness, in this case, he is thinking well of Allah, Allah will think well of him.

If a disciple is sick, tired, or lazy, he may even feel unable to move. However, he must show that he is strong and strives to overcome his own limitations. He should talk about the blessings of Allah, such as his body and the power he has given him. In doing so, Allah will give him strength to overcome his troubles. This approach can be applied to all aspects of life. For example, if someone fails in his business, if he works to show that he is succeeding, Allah may change the situation in a second.

Sidi Shaykh added that in this way, the person will become happy. He makes his Shaykh and the people around him happy. But if he is always crying about his situation, and complaining that he doesn't have anything, he will struggle more and more. Even if the listener makes *du'a* for him for an opening (*fath*) there will be no opening (*fath*). Even if Allah made an opening for him, as Allah is the All-Opening (*al-Fattah*), the person has already closed the door of opening for himself. He may not be able to see it if he doesn't have a positive and grateful mindset. Even if Allah provides sustenance in abundance, it may not reach the person. If he closes the doors of heaven, the doors of mercy will not be opened for him.

If a person truly believes that Allah has the power to elevate his situation from a lower state to a higher one, he will see his belief manifested in no time. The degree of one's belief in Allah is equivalent to the degree of the opening of the doors of mercy for him.

Sidi Shaykh mentioned that he experienced this with his disciples. There are those who have found themselves in a better situation because they knew how to listen to advice and apply it. And there are also those whose situations did not change because they listened but did not apply the advice, holding onto what they have and refusing to let go.

Sidi Shaykh gave the example of the Friday gathering at the beginning of the Tariqa. In the early days, only four people used to attend the Friday gathering. While there were suggestions to visit other zawiyas or tombs, Sidi Shaykh insisted on staying in the Zawiya and holding the gathering there because even if some only saw the gathering with four people, Sidi Shaykh saw it with four million. Today, the Tariqa has millions of disciples. Allah changed the situation due to positive thinking and having good expectations of Him.

Lecture 29.
March 23, 2023

*

The blessings of the *Wali*

Q: The blessings of the *Wali*.

In this lecture, Sidi Shaykh first spoke about the blessings (*barakah*) bestowed by the *Wali* when he visits a country or a place. He mentioned how in the past, people from different countries, such as countries in southern Africa for example, would invite one of the *Ahl al-Bayt*, peace be upon them, to live in their country. They would give him a house, marry him to their women, and offer him everything just to benefit from his blessings in their country. They would seek rain from Allah through his blessing. If they had an epidemic, they would ask Allah for healing, etc.

Thus, wherever the *Wali* goes, he spreads blessings. That's where al-Khidr got his name. His name refers to the fact that wherever he puts his foot, he brings sustenance, blessings, love, and everything good to that place. Sustenance isn't limited to material things like food but also includes sciences, knowledge, and health.

[Note: In Arabic, the word al-Khidr is a noun that shares the same root as the word green (*akhdar*).]

Sidi Shaykh added that if someone takes a *Wali* as his Shaykh, the main reason is to be brought from darkness to the Light of Allah. So reasonably, if he gets near the *Wali*, he is charged with that Light. In reality, it is not only him who gets replenished from the *Wali*, but also all the heavens and the earth, because Allah is the Light of the heavens and the earth, and the example of His Light, the niche, the lamp, the glass, and the shining star, are the *Wali* himself, which means that he is the source of all what is in the heavens and the earth.

Sidi Shaykh explained further and said that this Light (*nuraniyyah*) appeared on earth since Adam, peace be upon him. When the Prophet Muhammad ﷺ came up with the seal of Prophethood (*khatimiyyat-al-nubuwa*), he said: "The earth has been made a mosque for Me."[113] This is when the Light of the earth was completed, as before the Prophet ﷺ, it was limited to certain places on earth. After his seal (*khatmiyyah*), the entire earth became eligible for prayer, as its Light had been completed. The earth remained a mosque for the entire community of the Prophet ﷺ, but its Imams are the descendants of the Prophet ﷺ, the People of *Ahl al-Bayt*. That's why in the past, people used to bring one of

....

113 Al-Sijistani, Abu Dawud. *Sunan Abi Dawud*. #489.

Ahl al-Bayt to their countries because their land is a mosque but they needed an Imam.

Sidi Shaykh added that although the heavens and earth know their Imam, the problem lies with those who tread on the earth. Some of them understand; those are the ones who have been granted goodness from the Creator in advance and have become extinguished in their Lord. Others did not understand, and they are mentioned as disbelievers (*kuffar*) or hypocrites (*munafiqin*).

Sidi Shaykh also explained that the goodness bestowed by the Creator isn't just about material things like money. Hearing is sustenance, sight is sustenance. If Allah has made one's hearing and sight all Light, then he has sustained him.

*

The importance of remembrance

Q: The importance of remembrance.

Later in the lecture, Sidi Shaykh spoke about the importance of remembrance (*dhikr*). He said that if one makes his own house a mosque, he will be successful in this world (*dunya*) before the hereafter (*akhirah*). Sidi Shaykh explained that the intended meaning of "mosque" is an assembly of *dhikr*. The Prophet ﷺ said: "The assembly of *dhikr* is surrounded by angels."[114]

....

114 Al-'Asqalani, Ibn hajar. *Book 16.* #1540.

If there is *dhikr* in a house, either by the people living in the house or visitors, it will be surrounded by angels. The more there is *dhikr*, the more Allah will make this house known in the Supreme Assembly (*al-mala' al-'ala*), which is the highest assembly of angels and the closest to Allah. For example, if there was one hour of remembrance in the house, only the angels who were present at that hour would know. However, if *dhikr* was continuous, both the angels of the day and the angels of the night would know.

Sidi Shaykh added that everyone who enters a house for *dhikr* has ten angels with him. That's why a good deed is multiplied tenfold and a sin is recompensed with the same, because the angels pray for forgiveness for this person. Furthermore, the angels try to awaken this person from heedlessness, to make *istighfar* and repent, and if he repents, the sin will not be recorded.

Sidi Shaykh said that if ten people are engaging in *dhikr*, there are at least one hundred angels with them. And those one hundred angels have their own acquaintances in the spiritual realm, just as people do in the physical realm. Those angels love *dhikr*. In fact, they exist mainly to engage in praising Allah (*tasbih*), sanctifying Allah (*taqdis*), and praying upon the Prophet ﷺ, as Allah said in the Quran in surah al-Ahzab verse 56: **"Truly God and His angels invoke blessings upon the Prophet."**[115] And in Surah al-Baqara verse 30: **"While we hymn Thy praise and call Thee Holy."**[116]

....

115 Quran 33:56.
116 Quran 1:30.

Sidi Shaykh explained that if one prays on the Prophet ﷺ, he is descending what is happening in the spiritual realm, in reference to verse 56 of Surah al-Ahzab, to the physical realm. In doing so, he creates a link with the angels who are making *dhikr* with him. If it is more than one person, it becomes a mosque, an assembly of *dhikr*. One person is counted as one hundred, and one hundred is counted as one thousand, and so on.

Those angels have relationships with other angels, and they speak about this person's personality, spiritual aspiration (*himma*), and remembrance (*dhikr*). As a result, he becomes famous in the spiritual realm of the All-Merciful. The angels would say: "So-and-so is always in *dhikr* and so-and-so is one of the lovers of the Prophet ﷺ." These angels will seek forgiveness for the person, they will even pray for him and take him as an imam. This is valid for everyone who is in *dhikr* of Allah, but when it comes to the vicegerent (*khalifa*) of Allah or the representative of Allah on earth, it cannot be said that there are ten angels doing *dhikr* with him and that one reward is multiplied tenfold for him. The vicegerent represents the Light of the heavens and the earth. Therefore, when he sends prayers and blessings upon the Prophet ﷺ and engages in *dhikr*, the heavens, the earth, and all that they contain surround him. This is the vicegerent; the whole universe is aware of His existence. Sayyiduna Jibril, peace be upon him, performed the *adhan* in the heavens to announce that Allah loves this person, and thus, you should love him too. Here, Sayyiduna Jibril is addressing not just ten angels, but all the angels.

Allah will send down acceptance for him (*qubul*) on earth, and the people of the earth will love him, and they will come to him in groups. Only the lovers, the people of goodness, will come to him. As for the people of evil, they will fight against him. That is why his deeds are not counted as rewards multiplied by ten and that is why Allah divided religion into islam, faith (*iman*), excellence (*ihsan*).

Sidi Shaykh explained further using the example of fasting. He said that the only act of worship for which Allah did not specify a particular reward is fasting. The rule that one day of fasting equals ten days does not apply in this case, as Allah stated in a Hadith *Qudsi*: "Every good deed of Adam's son is for him except fasting; it is for Me. and I shall reward for it."[117] If a person forgets about food and water while working on the station of excellence, the station of vision, and becomes extinct in his Lord, then all of his time will become like fasting and Ramadan, and all of his nights will become like the Night of Decree (*laylat al-qadr*).

----

117 Al-Nasa'i, Ahmad. *Sunan al-Nasa'i.* #2219.

Lecture 30.
March, 2023

*

The companions' behavior with the Prophet ﷺ.

Q: The companions' behavior with the Prophet ﷺ.

Sidi Shaykh mentioned that when the Prophet ﷺ spoke, the companions believed in him without any need for discussion. They knew that all that he says is a revelation. Nowadays it has become different. When someone brings up a Hadith of the Prophet ﷺ, he may be told that the Hadith is weak or subject to doubts, and that this is an innovation (*bid'ah*).

Sidi Shaykh added that when a companion recounts a Hadith of the Prophet ﷺ, he cannot be mistaken. Perhaps in other matters, he could make errors, but not when it comes to the Prophet's ﷺ Hadith. Even the jews used to recount Hadiths of the Prophet without errors. Even his biggest enemies described him correctly.

*

The purity of *Ahl al-Bayt*

Q: A disciple cited the example of Abu Sufyan, who was once among the Prophet's ﷺ biggest enemies. When he was asked about the Prophet ﷺ, he perfectly described his greatness. Another disciple discussed the qualities of the Prophet and asked Sidi Shaykh how the Prophet ﷺ transmitted these qualities to *Ahl al-Bayt*.

Sidi Shaykh said that this fact cannot be denied, but the sanctity of the Prophet ﷺ is something that no one can reach. He then mentioned the Hadith *Qudsi* of when the Prophet ﷺ asked Allah, Prestigious and Majestic, about how He created him. Allah responded: "I took a part of my Light and I divided it into three parts, and the first part I created You from it O Muhammad and the people of your household (*ahlu baytuk*)"[118]. Allah did not specify that He created Muhammad ﷺ from the first part and *Ahl al-Bayt* from the second part, they are both created from the same part. This means that Muhammad ﷺ and *Ahl al-Bayt* are one.

Sidi Shaykh also mentioned the Hadith of the people of the cloak (*ahl al-kissa*), in which Sayyiduna Muhammad ﷺ gathered Sayyiduna Ali, Ummuna Fatima al-Zahra, Sayyiduna al-Hasan, and Sayyiduna al-Hussain under his cloak. When they were all under the cloak, they became one. Then the Prophet recited the verse: "**Allah only desires**

....

118 Al-Shafi'i, 'Abd al-Rahman. *Nuzhat al-Majalis*. Vol. 2, Page 96.

to keep away the uncleanness from you, O people of the House, and to purify you a thorough purifying."** Ummu Salama, the wife of the Prophet ﷺ, asked to enter with them under the cloak of the Prophet, he said to her: "You are better where you are."[119]

Umm Salama was in her house, which was the house of the Prophet ﷺ and *Ahl al-Bayt* were her guests. Typically, if someone is a guest and asked by the host to do something he will accept at least out of modesty. Thus, upon analyzing the scene, one can realize that there are no emotions involved as it is a revelation from Allah, and it remains unchanged.

Sidi Shaykh mentioned another Hadith *Qudsi* where Allah said: "I took one handful of My Light and said, 'Be Muhammad!'"[120] When someone hears this Hadith, he should not imagine that Sayyiduna Muhammad ﷺ was in that one handful of Light, and then *Ahl al-Bayt* were created. This is incorrect, as *Ahl al-Bayt* already existed in that one handful of Light, along with Sayyiduna Muhammad ﷺ. This is why the Prophet ﷺ used to call Ummuna Fatima al-Zahra "The mother of her father." This Hadith can be interpreted in two ways: first, it can be interpreted that Ummuna Fatima az-Zahara gave birth to the Prophet ﷺ as she is his mother, and second, it can be interpreted that Sayyiduna al-Hassan and Sayyiduna al-Hussain have both the degree of Prophets because Ummuna Fatima, their mother, is the mother of the Prophet ﷺ, and thus whoever she gave birth to is a Prophet.

....

119 *Jami' al-Tirmidhi* #3787.
120 Abu Zid, Fawzi Muhammad. *Al-Qawl al-Sadid*. Page 37.

Sidi Shaykh cited more Hadiths to explain that the Prophet ﷺ and *Ahl al-Bayt* cannot be separated. For example, when the Prophet ﷺ said to Sayyiduna Ali, peace be upon him: "Your Light is from My Light and My Light is from Your Light,"[121] and, "One who has me as his master has 'Ali as his master."[122]

Sidi Shaykh explained that the issue is that people are limited by the physical appearance of the *Ahl al-Bayt* and forget about their inner essence, which is the spirit. This is why Allah said to the Prophet ﷺ in Surah al-Isra verse 85: **"They ask thee about the Spirit. Say, 'The Spirit is from the Command of my Lord'."**[123] It does not mean that the Prophet ﷺ does not know what is the spirit or how the spirit descended in the body, He certainly knows. However, maybe those who are asking lack capacity and readiness to hear about the reality of the spirit.

From this perspective, the folk of Allah (*ahl Allah*) have a well-known saying: "Don't reveal it to those who don't deserve it, and don't conceal it from its people." Here, they are referring to Divine secrets.

Sidi Shaykh also referred to the saying of Abu Hurayra, peace be upon him: "I have memorized two vessels of knowledge from Allah's Messenger ﷺ. As for one of them, he informed me and I have propagated it to you. And as for the other, had I disclosed it, this throat would have been cut."

....

121 Al-Jouini, Ibrahim. *Fara'id al-Simtayin*. Vol. 1, page 40.
122 Ibn Hanbal, Ahmad. *Musnad* Ahmad. #961.
123 Quran 17:85.

Later in the lecture, Sidi Shaykh spoke about the Quran. He said that Allah is sending a message in the Quran, but people are limited to just reading and reciting it. For example, if someone sends a text message saying: "I am in a certain place, come and help me", a group of people receive the message and pass the phone to one another to read the message. They will keep reading it every day, but no one will go and help the person. No one understood the message, and it is the same with the Quran.

Sidi Shaykh added that the companions were verses of the Quran. Each of them is concerned with the revelation of some verses. Some have been the subject of verses of beauty (*jamal*), others are concerned with verses of majesty (*jalal*), and so on. The Prophet ﷺ said: "My companions are like the stars, whichever of them you follow, you will be rightly guided."[124] The companions are like letters of the Quran, representing the separation (*farq*) of the Quran. As for the Prophet ﷺ, he embodies the entirety of the Quran, and *Ahl al-Bayt* represent the secrets of the Quran. Sayyiduna Ali, may Allah honor his face, said: "I am the Dot".

....

124 Al-Suyuti, Jalal al-Din. *Takhrij Ahadith al-Shifa*. Page, 193.

Printed and bound
in Germany